THE YOGA SUTRAS OF PATANJALI

"THE BOOK OF THE SPIRITUAL MAN"

An Interpretation By
Charles Johnston

SASA PUBLISHING (OPC) PRIVATE LIMITED

THE YOGA SUTRAS OF PATANJALI

CHARLES JOHNSTON

REPUBLISHED IN 2026

PUBLISHED BY

SASA PUBLISHING (OPC) PRIVATE LIMITED

8-1, NEELITHOTTI KANDRIGA

SATYAVEDU – 517588, CHITOOR DISTRICT

ANDHRAPRADESH

Tel : 9441595078

sasapublishing@outlook.com

ISBN : 978-93-48584-70-0

THE YOGA SUTRAS OF PATANJALI

Contents

INTRODUCTION TO BOOK I

The Yoga Sutras of Patanjali are in themselves exceedingly brief, less than ten pages of large type in the original. Yet they contain the essence of practical wisdom, set forth in admirable order and detail. The theme, if the present interpreter be right, is the great regeneration, the birth of the spiritual from the psychical man: the same theme which Paul so wisely and eloquently set forth in writing to his disciples in Corinth, the theme of all mystics in all lands.

We think of ourselves as living a purely physical life, in these material bodies of ours. In reality, we have gone far indeed from pure physical life; for ages, our life has been psychical, we have been centred and immersed in the psychic nature. Some of the schools of India say that the psychic nature is, as it were, a looking-glass, wherein are mirrored the things seen by the physical eyes, and heard by the physical ears. But this is a magic mirror; the images remain, and take a certain life of their own. Thus within the psychic realm of our life there grows up an imaged world wherein we dwell; a world of the images of things seen and heard, and therefore a world of memories; a world also of hopes and desires, of fears and regrets. Mental life grows up among these images, built on a measuring and comparing, on the massing of images together into general ideas; on the abstraction of new notions and images from these; till a new world is built up within, full of desires and hates, ambition, envy, longing, speculation, curiosity, self-will, self-interest.

The teaching of the East is, that all these are true powers overlaid by false desires; that though in manifestation psychical, they are in essence spiritual; that the psychical man is the veil and prophecy of the spiritual man.

The purpose of life, therefore, is the realizing of that prophecy; the unveiling of the immortal man; the birth of the spiritual from the psychical, whereby we enter our divine inheritance and come to inhabit Eternity. This is, indeed, salvation, the purpose of all true religion, in all times.

Patanjali has in mind the spiritual man, to be born from the psychical. His purpose is, to set in order the practical means for the unveiling and regeneration, and to indicate the fruit, the glory and the power, of that new birth.

Through the Sutras of the first book, Patanjali is concerned with the first great problem, the emergence of the spiritual man from the veils and meshes of the psychic nature, the moods and vestures of the mental and emotional man. Later will come the consideration of the nature and powers of the spiritual man, once he stands clear of the psychic veils and trammels, and a view of the realms in which these new spiritual powers are to be revealed.

At this point may come a word of explanation. I have been asked why I use the word Sutras, for these rules of Patanjali's system, when the word Aphorism has been connected with them in our minds for a generation. The reason is this: the name Aphorism suggests, to me at least, a pithy sentence of very general application; a piece of proverbial wisdom that may be quoted in a good many sets of circumstance, and which will almost bear on its face the evidence of its truth. But with a Sutra the case is different. It comes from the same root as the word "sew," and means, indeed, a thread, suggesting, therefore, a close knit, consecutive chain of argument. Not only has each Sutra a definite place in the system, but further, taken out of this place, it will be almost meaningless, and will by no means be self-evident. So I have thought best to adhere to the original word. The Sutras of Patanjali are as closely knit together, as dependent on each other, as the propositions of Euclid, and can no more be taken out of their proper setting.

In the second part of the first book, the problem of the emergence of the spiritual man is further dealt with. We are led to the consideration of the barriers to his emergence, of the overcoming of the barriers, and of certain steps and stages in the ascent from the ordinary consciousness of practical life, to the finer, deeper, radiant consciousness of the spiritual man.

BOOK I

1. OM: Here follows Instruction in Union.

Union, here as always in the Scriptures of India, means union of the individual soul with the Oversoul; of the personal consciousness with the Divine Consciousness, whereby the mortal becomes immortal, and enters the Eternal. Therefore, salvation is, first, freedom from sin and the sorrow which comes from sin, and then a divine and eternal well-being, wherein the soul partakes of the being, the wisdom and glory of God.

2. Union, spiritual consciousness, is gained through control of the versatile psychic nature.

The goal is the full consciousness of the spiritual man, illumined by the Divine Light. Nothing except the obdurate resistance of the psychic nature keeps us back from the goal. The psychical powers are spiritual powers run wild, perverted, drawn from their proper channel. Therefore our first task is, to regain control of this perverted nature, to chasten, purify and restore the misplaced powers.

3. Then the Seer comes to consciousness in his proper nature.

Egotism is but the perversion of spiritual being. Ambition is the inversion of spiritual power. Passion is the distortion of love. The mortal is the limitation of the immortal. When these false images give place to true, then the spiritual man stands forth luminous, as the sun, when the clouds disperse.

4. Heretofore the Seer has been enmeshed in the activities of the psychic nature.

The power and life which are the heritage of the spiritual man have been caught and enmeshed in psychical activities. Instead of pure being in the Divine, there has been fretful, combative, egotism, its hand against every man. Instead of the light of pure vision, there have been restless senses nave been re and imaginings. Instead of spiritual joy, the undivided joy of pure being, there has been self-indulgence of body and mind. These are all real forces, but distorted from their true nature and goal. They must be extricated, like gems from the matrix, like the pith from the reed, steadily, without destructive violence. Spiritual powers are to be drawn forth from the psychic meshes.

5. The psychic activities are five; they are either subject or not subject to the five hindrances (Book II, 3).

The psychic nature is built up through the image-making power, the power which lies behind and dwells in mind-pictures. These pictures do not remain quiescent in the mind;

they are kinetic, restless, stimulating to new acts. Thus the mind-image of an indulgence suggests and invites to a new indulgence; the picture of past joy is framed in regrets or hopes. And there is the ceaseless play of the desire to know, to penetrate to the essence of things, to classify. This, too, busies itself ceaselessly with the mind-images. So that we may classify the activities of the psychic nature thus:

6. These activities are: Sound intellection, unsound intellection, predication, sleep, memory.

We have here a list of mental and emotional powers; of powers that picture and observe, and of powers that picture and feel. But the power to know and feel is spiritual and immortal. What is needed is, not to destroy it, but to raise it from the psychical to the spiritual realm.

7. The elements of sound intellection are: direct observation, inductive reason, and trustworthy testimony.

Each of these is a spiritual power, thinly veiled. Direct observation is the outermost form of the Soul's pure vision. Inductive reason rests on the great principles of continuity and correspondence; and these, on the supreme truth that all life is of the One. Trustworthy testimony, the sharing of one soul in the wisdom of another, rests on the ultimate oneness of all souls.

8. Unsound intellection is false understanding, not resting on a perception of the true nature of things.

When the object is not truly perceived, when the observation is inaccurate and faulty, thought or reasoning based on that mistaken perception is of necessity false and unsound.

9. Predication is carried on through words or thoughts not resting on an object perceived.

The purpose of this Sutra is, to distinguish between the mental process of predication, and observation, induction or testimony. Predication is the attribution of a quality or action to a subject, by adding to it a predicate. In the sentence, "the man is wise," "the man" is the subject; "is wise" is the predicate. This may be simply an interplay of thoughts, without the presence of the object thought of; or the things thought of may be imaginary or unreal; while observation, induction and testimony always go back to an object.

10. Sleep is the psychic condition which rests on mind states, all material things being absent.

In waking life, we have two currents of perception; an outer current of physical things seen and heard and perceived; an inner current of mind-images and thoughts. The outer current ceases in sleep; the inner current continues, and watching the mind-images float before the field of consciousness, we "dream." Even when there are no dreams, there is still a certain consciousness in sleep, so that, on waking, one says, "I have slept well," or "I have slept badly."

11. Memory is holding to mind-images of things perceived, without modifying them.

Here, as before, the mental power is explained in terms of mind-images, which are the material of which the psychic world is built, Therefore the sages teach that the world of our perception, which is indeed a world of mind-images, is but the wraith or shadow of the real and everlasting world. In this sense, memory is but the psychical inversion of the spiritual, ever-present vision. That which is ever before the spiritual eye of the Seer needs not to be remembered.

12. The control of these psychic activities comes through the right use of the will, and through ceasing from self-indulgence.

If these psychical powers and energies, even such evil things as passion and hate and fear, are but spiritual powers fallen and perverted, how are we to bring about their release and restoration? Two means are presented to us: the awakening of the spiritual will, and the purification of mind and thought.

13. The right use of the will is the steady, effort to stand in spiritual being.

We have thought of ourselves, perhaps, as creatures moving upon this earth, rather helpless, at the mercy of storm and hunger and our enemies. We are to think of ourselves as immortals, dwelling in the Light, encompassed and sustained by spiritual powers. The steady effort to hold this thought will awaken dormant and unrealized powers, which will unveil to us the nearness of the Eternal.

14. This becomes a firm resting-place, when followed long, persistently, with earnestness.

We must seek spiritual life in conformity with the laws of spiritual life, with earnestness, humility, gentle charity, which is an acknowledgment of the One Soul within us all. Only through obedience to that shared Life, through perpetual remembrance of our oneness with all Divine Being, our nothingness apart from Divine Being, can we enter our inheritance.

15. Ceasing from self-indulgence is conscious mastery over the thirst for sensuous pleasure here or hereafter.

Rightly understood, the desire for sensation is the desire of being, the distortion of the soul's eternal life. The lust of sensual stimulus and excitation rests on the longing to feel one's life keenly, to gain the sense of being really alive. This sense of true life comes only with the coming of the soul, and the soul comes only in silence, after self-indulgence has been courageously and loyally stilled, through reverence before the coming soul.

16. The consummation of this is freedom from thirst for any mode of psychical activity, through the establishment of the spiritual man.

In order to gain a true understanding of this teaching, study must be supplemented by devoted practice, faith by works. The reading of the words will not avail. There must be a real effort to stand as the Soul, a real ceasing from self-indulgence. With this awakening of the spiritual will, and purification, will come at once the growth of the spiritual man and our awakening consciousness as the spiritual man; and this, attained in even a small degree, will help us notably in our contest. To him that hath, shall be given.

17. Meditation with an object follows these stages: first, exterior examining, then interior judicial action, then joy, then realization of individual being.

In the practice of meditation, a beginning may be made by fixing the attention upon some external object, such as a sacred image or picture, or a part of a book of devotion. In the second stage, one passes from the outer object to an inner pondering upon its lessons. The third stage is the inspiration, the heightening of the spiritual will, which results from this pondering. The fourth stage is the realization of one's spiritual being, as enkindled by this meditation.

18. After the exercise of the will has stilled the psychic activities, meditation rests only on the fruit of former meditations.

In virtue of continued practice and effort, the need of an external object on which to rest the meditation is outgrown. An interior state of spiritual consciousness is reached, which is called "the cloud of things knowable" (Book IV, 29).

19. Subjective consciousness arising from a natural cause is possessed by those who have laid aside their bodies and been absorbed into subjective nature.

Those who have died, entered the paradise between births, are in a condition resembling meditation without an external object. But in the fullness of time, the seeds of desire in them will spring up, and they will be born again into this world.

20. For the others, there is spiritual consciousness, led up to by faith, valour, right mindfulness, one-pointedness, perception.

It is well to keep in mind these steps on the path to illumination: faith, valour, right mindfulness, one-pointedness, perception. Not one can be dispensed with; all must be won. First faith; and then from faith, valour; from valour, right mindfulness; from right mindfulness, a one-pointed aspiration toward the soul; from this, perception; and finally, full vision as the soul.

21. Spiritual consciousness is nearest to those of keen, intense will.

The image used is the swift impetus of the torrent; the kingdom must be taken by force. Firm will comes only through effort; effort is inspired by faith. The great secret is this: it is not enough to have intuitions; we must act on them; we must live them.

22. The will may be weak, or of middle strength, or intense.

Therefore there is a spiritual consciousness higher than this. For those of weak will, there is this counsel: to be faithful in obedience, to live the life, and thus to strengthen the will to more perfect obedience. The will is not ours, but God's, and we come into it only through obedience. As we enter into the spirit of God, we are permitted to share the power of God.

Higher than the three stages of the way is the goal, the end of the way.

23. Or spiritual consciousness may be gained by ardent service of the Master.

If we think of our lives as tasks laid on us by the Master of Life, if we look on all duties as parts of that Master's work, entrusted to us, and forming our life-work; then, if we obey, promptly, loyally, sincerely, we shall enter by degrees into the Master's life and share the Master's power. Thus we shall be initiated into the spiritual will.

24. The Master is the spiritual man, who is free from hindrances, bondage to works, and the fruition and seed of works.

The Soul of the Master, the Lord, is of the same nature as the soul in us; but we still bear the burden of many evils, we are in bondage through our former works, we are under the dominance of sorrow. The Soul of the Master is free from sin and servitude and sorrow.

25. In the Master is the perfect seed of Omniscience.

The Soul of the Master is in essence one with the Oversoul, and therefore partaker of the Oversoul's all-wisdom and all-power. All spiritual attainment rests on this, and is possible because the soul and the Oversoul are One.

26. He is the Teacher of all who have gone before, since he is not limited by Time.

From the beginning, the Oversoul has been the Teacher of all souls, which, by their entrance into the Oversoul, by realizing their oneness with the Oversoul, have inherited the kingdom of the Light. For the Oversoul is before Time, and Time, father of all else, is one of His children.

27. His word is OM.

OM: the symbol of the Three in One, the three worlds in the Soul; the three times, past, present, future, in Eternity; the three Divine Powers, Creation, Preservation, Transformation, in the one Being; the three essences, immortality, omniscience, joy, in the one Spirit. This is the Word, the Symbol, of the Master and Lord, the perfected Spiritual Man.

28. Let there be soundless repetition of OM and meditation thereon.

This has many meanings, in ascending degrees. There is, first, the potency of the word itself, as of all words. Then there is the manifold significance of the symbol, as suggested above. Lastly, there is the spiritual realization of the high essences thus symbolized. Thus we rise step by step to the Eternal.

29. Thence come the awakening of interior consciousness, and the removal of barriers.

Here again faith must be supplemented by works, the life must be led as well as studied, before the full meaning can be understood. The awakening of spiritual consciousness can only be understood in measure as it is entered. It can only be entered where the conditions are present: purity of heart, and strong aspiration, and the resolute conquest of each sin.

This, however, may easily be understood: that the recognition of the three worlds as resting in the Soul leads us to realize ourselves and all life as of the Soul; that, as we dwell, not in past, present or future, but in the Eternal, we become more at one with the Eternal; that, as we view all organization, preservation, mutation as the work of the Divine One, we shall come more into harmony with the One, and thus remove the barrier' in our path toward the Light.

In the second part of the first book, the problem of the emergence of the spiritual man is further dealt with. We are led to the consideration of the barriers to his emergence, of the overcoming of the barriers, and of certain steps and stages in the ascent from the ordinary consciousness of practical life, to the finer, deeper, radiant consciousness of the spiritual man.

30. The barriers to interior consciousness, which drive the psychic nature this way and that, are these: sickness, inertia, doubt, lightmindedness, laziness, intemperance, false notions, inability to reach a stage of meditation, or to hold it when reached.

We must remember that we are considering the spiritual man as enwrapped and enmeshed by the psychic nature, the emotional and mental powers; and as unable to come to clear consciousness, unable to stand and see clearly, because of the psychic veils of the personality. Nine of these are enumerated, and they go pretty thoroughly into the brute toughness of the psychic nature.

Sickness is included rather for its effect on the emotions and mind, since bodily infirmity, such as blindness or deafness, is no insuperable barrier to spiritual life, and may sometimes be a help, as cutting off distractions. It will be well for us to ponder over each of these nine activities, thinking of each as a psychic state, a barrier to the interior consciousness of the spiritual man.

31. Grieving, despondency, bodily restlessness, the drawing in and sending forth of the life-breath also contribute to drive the psychic nature to and fro.

The first two moods are easily understood. We can well see bow a sodden psychic condition, flagrantly opposed to the pure and positive joy of spiritual life, would be a barrier. The next, bodily restlessness, is in a special way the fault of our day and generation. When it is conquered, mental restlessness will be half conquered, too.

The next two terms, concerning the life breath, offer some difficulty. The surface meaning is harsh and irregular breathing; the deeper meaning is a life of harsh and irregular impulses.

32. Steady application to a principle is the way to put a stop to these.

The will, which, in its pristine state, was full of vigour, has been steadily corrupted by self-indulgence, the seeking of moods and sensations for sensation's sake. Hence come all the morbid and sickly moods of the mind. The remedy is a return to the pristine state of the will, by vigorous, positive effort; or, as we are here told, by steady application to a principle. The principle to which we should thus steadily apply ourselves should be one arising from the reality of spiritual life; valorous work for the soul, in others as in ourselves.

33. By sympathy with the happy, compassion for the sorrowful, delight in the holy, disregard of the unholy, the psychic nature moves to gracious peace.

When we are wrapped up in ourselves, shrouded with the cloak of our egotism, absorbed in our pains and bitter thoughts, we are not willing to disturb or strain our own sickly mood by giving kindly sympathy to the happy, thus doubling their joy, or by showing compassion for the sad, thus halving their sorrow. We refuse to find delight in holy things, and let the mind brood in sad pessimism on unholy things. All these evil psychic moods must be conquered by strong effort of will. This rending of the veils will reveal to us something of the grace and peace which are of the interior consciousness of the spiritual man.

34. Or peace may be reached by the even sending forth and control of the life-breath.

Here again we may look for a double meaning: first, that even and quiet breathing which is a part of the victory over bodily restlessness; then the even and quiet tenor of life, without harsh or dissonant impulses, which brings stillness to the heart.

35. Faithful, persistent application to any object, if completely attained, will bind the mind to steadiness.

We are still considering how to overcome the wavering and perturbation of the psychic nature, which make it quite unfit to transmit the inward consciousness and stillness. We are once more told to use the will, and to train it by steady and persistent work: by "sitting close" to our work, in the phrase of the original.

36. As also will a joyful, radiant spirit.

There is no such illusion as gloomy pessimism, and it has been truly said that a man's cheerfulness is the measure of his faith. Gloom, despondency, the pale cast of thought, are very amenable to the will. Sturdy and courageous effort will bring a clear and valorous mind. But it must always be remembered that this is not for solace to the personal man, but is rather an offering to the ideal of spiritual life, a contribution to the universal and universally shared treasure in heaven.

37. Or the purging of self-indulgence from the psychic nature.

We must recognize that the fall of man is a reality, exemplified in our own persons. We have quite other sins than the animals, and far more deleterious; and they have all come through self-indulgence, with which our psychic natures are soaked through and through. As we climbed down hill for our pleasure, so must we climb up again for our purification and restoration to our former high estate. The process is painful, perhaps, yet indispensable.

38. Or a pondering on the perceptions gained in dreams and dreamless sleep.

For the Eastern sages, dreams are, it is true, made up of images of waking life, reflections of what the eyes have seen and the ears heard. But dreams are something more, for the images are in a sense real, objective on their own plane; and the knowledge that there is another world, even a dreamworld, lightens the tyranny of material life. Much of poetry and art is such a solace from dreamland. But there is more in dream, for it may image what is above, as well as what is below; not only the children of men, but also the children by the shore of the immortal sea that brought us hither, may throw their images on this magic mirror: so, too, of the secrets of dreamless sleep with its pure vision, in even greater degree.

39. Or meditative brooding on what is dearest to the heart.

Here is a thought which our own day is beginning to grasp: that love is a form of knowledge; that we truly know any thing or any person, by becoming one therewith, in love. Thus love has a wisdom that the mind cannot claim, and by this hearty love, this becoming one with what is beyond our personal borders, we may take a long step toward freedom. Two directions for this may be suggested: the pure love of the artist for his work, and the earnest, compassionate search into the hearts of others.

40. Thus he masters all, from the atom to the Infinite.

Newton was asked how he made his discoveries. By intending my mind on them, he replied. This steady pressure, this becoming one with what we seek to understand, whether it be atom or soul, is the one means to know. When we become a thing, we really know it, not otherwise. Therefore live the life, to know the doctrine; do the will of the Father, if you would know the Father.

41. When the perturbations of the psychic nature have all been stilled, then the consciousness, like a pure crystal, takes the colour of what it rests on, whether that be the perceiver, perceiving, or the thing perceived.

This is a fuller expression of the last Sutra, and is so lucid that comment can hardly add to it. Everything is either perceiver, perceiving, or the thing perceived; or, as we might say, consciousness, force, or matter. The sage tells us that the one key will unlock the secrets of all three, the secrets of consciousness, force and matter alike. The thought is, that the cordial sympathy of a gentle heart, intuitively understanding the hearts of others, is really a manifestation of the same power as that penetrating perception whereby one divines the secrets of planetary motions or atomic structure.

42. When the consciousness, poised in perceiving, blends together the name, the object dwelt on and the idea, this is perception with exterior consideration.

In the first stage of the consideration of an external object, the perceiving mind comes to it, preoccupied by the name and idea conventionally associated with that object. For example, in coming to the study of a book, we think of the author, his period, the school to which he belongs. The second stage, set forth in the next Sutra, goes directly to the spiritual meaning of the book, setting its traditional trappings aside and finding its application to our own experience and problems.

The commentator takes a very simple illustration: a cow, where one considers, in the first stage, the name of the cow, the animal itself and the idea of a cow in the mind. In the second stage, one pushes these trappings aside and, entering into the inmost being of the cow, shares its consciousness, as do some of the artists who paint cows. They get at the very life of what they study and paint.

43. When the object dwells in the mind, clear of memory-pictures, uncoloured by the mind, as a pure luminous idea, this is perception without exterior or consideration.

We are still considering external, visible objects. Such perception as is here described is of the nature of that penetrating vision whereby Newton, intending his mind on things, made his discoveries, or that whereby a really great portrait painter pierces to the soul of him whom he paints, and makes that soul live on canvas. These stages of perception are described in this way, to lead the mind up to an understanding of the piercing soul-vision of the spiritual man, the immortal.

44. The same two steps, when referring to things of finer substance, are said to be with, or without, judicial action of the mind.

We now come to mental or psychical objects: to images in the mind. It is precisely by comparing, arranging and superposing these mind-images that we get our general notions or concepts. This process of analysis and synthesis, whereby we select certain qualities in a group of mind-images, and then range together those of like quality, is the judicial action of the mind spoken of. But when we exercise swift divination upon the mind images, as does a poet or a man of genius, then we use a power higher than the judicial, and one nearer to the keen vision of the spiritual man.

45. Subtle substance rises in ascending degrees, to that pure nature which has no distinguishing mark.

As we ascend from outer material things which are permeated by separateness, and whose chief characteristic is to be separate, just as so many pebbles are separate from each other; as we ascend, first, to mind-images, which overlap and coalesce in both space and time, and then to ideas and principles, we finally come to purer essences, drawing ever nearer and nearer to unity.

Or we may illustrate this principle thus. Our bodily, external selves are quite distinct and separate, in form, name, place, substance; our mental selves, of finer substance, meet and part, meet and part again, in perpetual concussion and interchange; our spiritual selves attain true consciousness through unity, where the partition wall between us and the Highest, between us and others, is broken down and we are all made perfect in the One. The highest riches are possessed by all pure souls, only when united. Thus we rise from separation to true individuality in unity.

46. The above are the degrees of limited and conditioned spiritual consciousness, still containing the seed of separateness.

In the four stages of perception above described, the spiritual vision is still working through the mental and psychical, the inner genius is still expressed through the outer, personal man. The spiritual man has yet to come completely to consciousness as himself, in his own realm, the psychical veils laid aside.

47. When pure perception without judicial action of the mind is reached, there follows the gracious peace of the inner self.

We have instanced certain types of this pure perception: the poet's divination, whereby he sees the spirit within the symbol, likeness in things unlike, and beauty in all things; the pure insight of the true philosopher, whose vision rests not on the appearances of life, but on its realities; or the saint's firm perception of spiritual life and being. All these are far advanced on the way; they have drawn near to the secret dwelling of peace.

48. In that peace, perception is unfailingly true.

The poet, the wise philosopher and the saint not only reach a wide and luminous consciousness, but they gain certain knowledge of substantial reality. When we know, we know that we know. For we have come to the stage where we know things by being them, and nothing can be more true than being. We rest on the rock, and know it to be rock, rooted in the very heart of the world.

49. The object of this perception is other than what is learned from the sacred books, or by sound inference, since this perception is particular.

The distinction is a luminous and inspiring one. The Scriptures teach general truths, concerning universal spiritual life and broad laws, and inference from their teaching is not less general. But the spiritual perception of the awakened Seer brings particular truth concerning his own particular life and needs, whether these be for himself or others. He receives defined, precise knowledge, exactly applying to what he has at heart.

50. The impress on the consciousness springing from this perception supersedes all previous impressions.

Each state or field of the mind, each field of knowledge, so to speak, which is reached by mental and emotional energies, is a psychical state, just as the mind picture of a stage with the actors on it, is a psychical state or field. When the pure vision, as of the poet, the philosopher, the saint, fills the whole field, all lesser views and visions are crowded out. This high consciousness displaces all lesser consciousness. Yet, in a certain sense, that which is viewed as part, even by the vision of a sage, has still an element of illusion, a thin psychical veil, however pure and luminous that veil may be. It is the last and highest psychic state.

51. When this impression ceases, then, since all impressions have ceased, there arises pure spiritual consciousness, with no seed of separateness left.

The last psychic veil is drawn aside, and the spiritual man stands with unveiled vision, pure serene.

INTRODUCTION TO BOOK II

The first book of Patanjali's Yoga Sutras is called the Book of Spiritual Consciousness. The second book, which we now begin, is the Book of the Means of Soul Growth. And we must remember that soul growth here means the growth of the realization of the spiritual man, or, to put the matter more briefly, the growth of the spiritual man, and the disentangling of the spiritual man from the wrappings, the veils, the disguises laid upon him by the mind and the psychical nature, wherein he is enmeshed, like a bird caught in a net.

The question arises: By what means may the spiritual man be freed from these psychical meshes and disguises, so that he may stand forth above death, in his radiant eternalness and divine power? And the second book sets itself to answer this very question, and to detail the means in a way entirely practical and very lucid, so that he who runs may read, and he who reads may understand and practise.

The second part of the second book is concerned with practical spiritual training, that is, with the earlier practical training of the spiritual man.

The most striking thing in it is the emphasis laid on the Commandments, which are precisely those of the latter part of the Decalogue, together with obedience to the Master. Our day and generation is far too prone to fancy that there can be mystical life and growth on some other foundation, on the foundation, for example, of intellectual curiosity or psychical selfishness. In reality, on this latter foundation the life of the spiritual man can never be built; nor, indeed, anything but a psychic counterfeit, a dangerous delusion.

Therefore Patanjali, like every great spiritual teacher, meets the question: What must I do to be saved? with the age-old answer: Keep the Commandments. Only after the disciple can say, These have I kept, can there be the further and finer teaching of the spiritual Rules.

It is, therefore, vital for us to realize that the Yoga system, like every true system of spiritual teaching, rests on this broad and firm foundation of honesty, truth, cleanness, obedience. Without these, there is no salvation; and he who practices these, even though ignorant of spiritual things, is laying up treasure against the time to come.

BOOK II

1. The practices which make for union with the Soul are: fervent aspiration, spiritual reading, and complete obedience to the Master.

The word which I have rendered "fervent aspiration" means primarily "fire"; and, in the Eastern teaching, it means the fire which gives life and light, and at the same time the fire which purifies. We have, therefore, as our first practice, as the first of the means of spiritual growth, that fiery quality of the will which enkindles and illumines, and, at the same time, the steady practice of purification, the burning away of all known impurities. Spiritual reading is so universally accepted and understood, that it needs no comment. The very study of Patanjali's Sutras is an exercise in spiritual reading, and a very effective one. And so with all other books of the Soul. Obedience to the Master means, that we shall make the will of the Master our will, and shall confirm in all wave to the will of the Divine, setting aside the wills of self, which are but psychic distortions of the one Divine Will. The constant effort to obey in all the ways we know and understand, will reveal new ways and new tasks, the evidence of new growth of the Soul. Nothing will do more for the spiritual man in us than this, for there is no such regenerating power as the awakening spiritual will.

2. Their aim is, to bring soul-vision, and to wear away hindrances.

The aim of fervour, spiritual reading and obedience to the Master, is, to bring soulvision, and to wear away hindrances. Or, to use the phrase we have already adopted, the aim of these practices is, to help the spiritual man to open his eyes; to help him also to throw aside the veils and disguises, the enmeshing psychic nets which surround him, tying his hands, as it were, and bandaging his eyes. And this, as all teachers testify, is a long and arduous task, a steady up-hill fight, demanding fine courage and persistent toil. Fervour, the fire of the spiritual will, is, as we said, two-fold: it illumines, and so helps the spiritual man to see; and it also burns up the nets and meshes which ensnare the spiritual man. So with the other means, spiritual reading and obedience. Each, in its action, is two-fold, wearing away the psychical, and upbuilding the spiritual man.

3. These are the hindrances: the darkness of unwisdom, self-assertion, lust hate, attachment.

Let us try to translate this into terms of the psychical and spiritual man. The darkness of unwisdom is, primarily, the self-absorption of the psychical man, his complete preoccupation with his own hopes and fears, plans and purposes, sensations and desires; so that he fails to see, or refuses to see, that there is a spiritual man; and so doggedly resists all efforts of the spiritual man to cast off his psychic tyrant and set himself free. This is the real darkness; and all those who deny the immortality of the soul, or deny the soul's existence, and so lay out their lives wholly for the psychical, mortal man and his ambitions, are under this power of darkness. Born of this darkness, this psychic self-absorption, is the dogged conviction that the psychic, personal man has separate, exclusive interests, which he can follow for himself alone; and this conviction, when put into practice in our life, leads to contest with other personalities, and so to hate. This hate, again, makes against the spiritual man, since it hinders the revelation of the high harmony between the spiritual man and his other selves, a harmony to be revealed only through the practice of love, that perfect love which casts out fear.

In like manner, lust is the psychic man's craving for the stimulus of sensation, the din of which smothers the voice of the spiritual man, as, in Shakespeare's phrase, the cackling geese would drown the song of the nightingale. And this craving for stimulus is the fruit of weakness, coming from the failure to find strength in the primal life of the spiritual man.

Attachment is but another name for psychic self-absorption; for we are absorbed, not in outward things, but rather in their images within our minds; our inner eyes are fixed on them; our inner desires brood over them; and em we blind ourselves to the presence of the prisoner' the enmeshed and fettered spiritual man.

4. The darkness of unwisdom is the field of the others. These hindrances may be dormant, or worn thin, or suspended, or expanded.

Here we have really two Sutras in one. The first has been explained already: in the darkness of unwisdom grow the parasites, hate, lust, attachment. They are all outgrowths of the self-absorption of the psychical self.

Next, we are told that these barriers may be either dormant, or suspended, or expanded, or worn thin. Faults which are dormant will be brought out through the pressure of life, or through the pressure of strong aspiration. Thus expanded, they must be fought and conquered, or, as Patanjali quaintly says, they must be worn thin,-as a veil might, or the links of manacles.

5 The darkness of ignorance is: holding that which is unenduring, impure, full of pain, not the Soul, to be eternal, pure, full of joy, the Soul.

This we have really considered already. The psychic man is unenduring, impure, full of pain, not the Soul, not the real Self. The spiritual man is enduring, pure, full of joy, the real Self. The darkness of unwisdom is, therefore, the self-absorption of the psychical, personal man, to the exclusion of the spiritual man. It is the belief, carried into action, that the personal man is the real man, the man for whom we should toil, for whom we should build, for whom we should live. This is that psychical man of whom it is said: he that soweth to the flesh, shall of the flesh reap corruption.

6. Self-assertion comes from thinking of the Seer and the instrument of vision as forming one self.

This is the fundamental idea of the Sankhya philosophy, of which the Yoga is avowedly the practical side. To translate this into our terms, we may say that the Seer is the spiritual man; the instrument of vision is the psychical man, through which the spiritual man gains experience of the outer world. But we turn the servant into the master. We attribute to the psychical man, the personal self, a reality which really belongs to the spiritual man alone; and so, thinking of the quality of the spiritual man as belonging to the psychical, we merge the spiritual man in the psychical; or, as the text says, we think of the two as forming one self.

7. Lust is the resting in the sense of enjoyment.

This has been explained again and again. Sensation, as, for example, the sense of taste, is meant to be the guide to action; in this case, the choice of wholesome food, and the avoidance of poisonous and hurtful things. But if we rest in the sense of taste, as a pleasure in itself; rest, that is, in the psychical side of taste, we fall into gluttony, and live to eat, instead of eating to live. So with the other great organic power, the power of reproduction. This lust comes into being, through resting in the sensation, and looking for pleasure from that.

8. Hate is the resting in the sense of pain.

Pain comes, for the most part, from the strife of personalities, the jarring discords between psychic selves, each of which deems itself supreme. A dwelling on this pain breeds hate, which tears the warring selves yet further asunder, and puts new enmity between them, thus hindering the harmony of the Real, the reconciliation through the Soul.

9. Attachment is the desire toward life, even in the wise, carried forward by its own energy.

The life here desired is the psychic life, the intensely vibrating life of the psychical self. This prevails even in those who have attained much wisdom, so long as it falls short of the wisdom of complete renunciation, complete obedience to each least behest of the spiritual man, and of the Master who guards and aids the spiritual man.

The desire of sensation, the desire of psychic life, reproduces itself, carried on by its own energy and momentum; and hence comes the circle of death and rebirth, death and rebirth, instead of the liberation of the spiritual man.

10. These hindrances, when they have become subtle, are to be removed by a countercurrent.

The darkness of unwisdom is to be removed by the light of wisdom, pursued through fervour, spiritual reading of holy teachings and of life itself, and by obedience to the Master.

Lust is to be removed by pure aspiration of spiritual life, which, bringing true strength and stability, takes away the void of weakness which we try to fill by the stimulus of sensations.

Hate is to be overcome by love. The fear that arises through the sense of separate, warring selves is to be stilled by the realization of the One Self, the one soul in all. This realization is the perfect love that casts out fear.

The hindrances are said to have become subtle when, by initial efforts, they have been located and recognized in the psychic nature.

11. Their active turnings are to be removed by meditation.

Here is, in truth, the whole secret of Yoga, the science of the soul. The active turnings, the strident vibrations, of selfishness, lust and hate are to be stilled by meditation, by letting heart and mind dwell in spiritual life, by lifting up the heart to the strong, silent life above, which rests in the stillness of eternal love, and needs no harsh vibration to convince it of true being.

12. The burden of bondage to sorrow has its root in these hindrances. It will be felt in this life, or in a life not yet manifested.

The burden of bondage to sorrow has its root in the darkness of unwisdom, in selfishness, in lust, in hate, in attachment to sensation. All these are, in the last analysis, absorption in the psychical self; and this means sorrow, because it means the sense of separateness, and this means jarring discord and inevitable death. But the psychical self will breed a new psychical self, in a new birth, and so new sorrows in a life not yet manifest.

13. From this root there grow and ripen the fruits of birth, of the life-span, of all that is tasted in life.

Fully to comment on this, would be to write a treatise on Karma and its practical working in detail, whereby the place and time of the next birth, its content and duration, are determined; and to do this the present commentator is in no wise fitted. But this much is clearly understood: that, through a kind of spiritual gravitation, the incarnating self is drawn to a home and life-circle which will give it scope and discipline; and its need of discipline is clearly conditioned by its character, its standing, its accomplishment.

14. These bear fruits of rejoicing, or of affliction, as they are sprung from holy or unholy works.

Since holiness is obedience to divine law, to the law of divine harmony, and obedience to harmony strengthens that harmony in the soul, which is the one true joy, therefore joy comes of holiness: comes, indeed, in no other way. And as unholiness is disobedience, and therefore discord, therefore unholiness makes for pain; and this two-fold law is true, whether the cause take effect in this, or in a yet unmanifested birth.

15. To him who possesses discernment, all personal life is misery, because it ever waxes and wanes, is ever afflicted with restlessness, makes ever new dynamic impresses in the mind; and because all its activities war with each other.

The whole life of the psychic self is misery, because it ever waxes and wanes; because birth brings inevitable death; because there is no expectation without its shadow, fear. The life of the psychic self is misery, because it is afflicted with restlessness; so that he who has much, finds not satisfaction, but rather the whetted hunger for more. The fire is not quenched by pouring oil on it; so desire is not quenched by the satisfaction of desire. Again, the life of the psychic self is misery, because it makes ever new dynamic impresses in the mind; because a desire satisfied is but the seed from which springs the desire to find like satisfaction again. The appetite comes in eating, as the proverb says, and grows by what it feeds on. And the psychic self, torn with conflicting desires, is ever the house divided against itself, which must surely fall.

16. This pain is to be warded off, before it has come.

In other words, we cannot cure the pains of life by laying on them any balm. We must cut the root, absorption in the psychical self. So it is said, there is no cure for the misery of longing, but to fix the heart upon the eternal.

17. The cause of what is to be warded off, is the absorption of the Seer in things seen.

Here again we have the fundamental idea of the Sankhya, which is the intellectual counterpart of the Yoga system. The cause of what is to be warded off, the root of misery, is the absorption of consciousness in the psychical man and the things which beguile the psychical man. The cure is liberation.

18. Things seen have as their property manifestation, action, inertia. They form the basis of the elements and the sense-powers. They make for experience and for liberation.

Here is a whole philosophy of life. Things seen, the total of the phenomena, possess as their property, manifestation, action, inertia: the qualities of force and matter in combination. These, in their grosser form, make the material world; in their finer, more subjective form, they make the psychical world, the world of sense-impressions and mind-images. And through this totality of the phenomenal, the soul gains experience, and is prepared for liberation. In other words, the whole outer world exists for the purposes of the soul, and finds in this its true reason for being.

19. The grades or layers of the Three Potencies are the defined, the undefined, that with distinctive mark, that without distinctive mark.

Or, as we might say, there are two strata of the physical, and two strata of the psychical realms. In each, there is the side of form, and the side of force. The form side of the physical is here called the defined. The force side of the physical is the undefined, that which has no boundaries. So in the psychical; there is the form side; that with distinctive marks, such as the characteristic features of mind-images; and there is the force side, without distinctive marks, such as the forces of desire or fear, which may flow now to this mind-image, now to that.

20. The Seer is pure vision. Though pure, he looks out through the vesture of the mind.

The Seer, as always, is the spiritual man whose deepest consciousness is pure vision, the pure life of the eternal. But the spiritual man, as yet unseeing in his proper person, looks out on the world through the eyes of the psychical man, by whom he is enfolded and enmeshed. The task is, to set this prisoner free, to clear the dust of ages from this buried temple.

21. The very essence of things seen is, that they exist for the Seer.

The things of outer life, not only material things, but the psychic man also, exist in very deed for the purposes of the Seer, the Soul, the spiritual man Disaster comes, when the psychical man sets up, so to speak, on his own account, trying to live for himself alone, and taking material things to solace his loneliness.

22. Though fallen away from him who has reached the goal, things seen have not alto fallen away, since they still exist for others.

When one of us conquers hate, hate does not thereby cease out of the world, since others still hate and suffer hatred. So with other delusions, which hold us in bondage to material things, and through which we look at all material things. When the coloured veil of illusion is gone, the world which we saw through it is also gone, for now we see life as it is, in the white radiance of eternity. But for others the coloured veil remains, and therefore the world thus coloured by it remains for them, and will remain till they, too, conquer delusion.

23. The association of the Seer with things seen is the cause of the realizing of the nature of things seen, and also of the realizing of the nature of the Seer.

Life is educative. All life's infinite variety is for discipline, for the development of the soul. So passing through many lives, the Soul learns the secrets of the world, the august laws that are written in the form of the snow-crystal or the majestic order of the stars. Yet all these laws are but reflections, but projections outward, of the laws of the soul; therefore in learning these, the soul learns to know itself. All life is but the mirror wherein the Soul learns to know its own face.

24. The cause of this association is the darkness of unwisdom.

The darkness of unwisdom is the absorption of consciousness in the personal life, and in the things seen by the personal life. This is the fall, through which comes experience, the learning of the lessons of life. When they are learned, the day of redemption is at hand.

25. The bringing of this association to an end, by bringing the darkness of unwisdom to an end, is the great liberation; this is the Seer's attainment of his own pure being.

When the spiritual man has, through the psychical, learned all life's lessons, the time has come for him to put off the veil and disguise of the psychical and to stand revealed a King, in the house of the Father. So shall he enter into his kingdom, and go no more out.

26. A discerning which is carried on without wavering is the means of liberation.

Here we come close to the pure Vedanta, with its discernment between the eternal and the temporal. St. Paul, following after Philo and Plato, lays down the same fundamental principle: the things seen are temporal, the things unseen are eternal.

Patanjali means something more than an intellectual assent, though this too is vital. He has in view a constant discriminating in act as well as thought; of the two ways which present themselves for every deed or choice, always to choose the higher way, that which makes for the things eternal: honesty rather than roguery, courage and not cowardice, the things of another rather than one's own, sacrifice and not indulgence. This true discernment, carried out constantly, makes for liberation.

27. His illuminations is sevenfold, rising In successive stages.

Patanjali's text does not tell us what the seven stages of this illumination are. The commentator thus describes them:

First, the danger to be escaped is recognized; it need not be recognized a second time. Second, the causes of the danger to be escaped are worn away; they need not be worn away a second time. Third, the way of escape is clearly perceived, by the contemplation which checks psychic perturbation. Fourth, the means of escape, clear discernment, has been developed. This is the fourfold release belonging to insight. The final release from the psychic is three-fold: As fifth of the seven degrees, the dominance of its thinking is ended; as sixth, its potencies, like rocks from a precipice, fall of themselves; once dissolved, they do not grow again. Then, as seventh, freed from these potencies, the spiritual man stands forth in his own nature as purity and light. Happy is the spiritual man who beholds this seven-fold illumination in its ascending stages.

28. From steadfastly following after the means of Yoga, until impurity is worn away, there comes the illumination of thought up to full discernment.

Here, we enter on the more detailed practical teaching of Patanjali, with its sound and luminous good sense. And when we come to detail the means of Yoga, we may well be astonished at their simplicity. There is little in them that is mysterious. They are very familiar. The essence of the matter lies in carrying them out.

29. The eight means of Yoga are: the Commandments, the Rules, right Poise, right Control of the life-force, Withdrawal, Attention, Meditation, Contemplation.

These eight means are to be followed in their order, in the sense which will immediately be made clear. We can get a ready understanding of the first two by comparing them with the Commandments which must be obeyed by all good citizens, and the Rules which are laid on the members of religious orders. Until one has fulfilled the first, it is futile to concern oneself with the second. And so with all the means of Yoga. They must be taken in their order.

30. The Commandments are these: nom injury, truthfulness, abstaining from stealing, from impurity, from covetousness.

These five precepts are almost exactly the same as the Buddhist Commandments: not to kill, not to steal, not to be guilty of incontinence, not to drink intoxicants, to speak the truth. Almost identical is St. Paul's list: Thou shalt not commit adultery, thou shalt not kill, thou shalt not steal, thou shalt not covet. And in the same spirit is the answer made to the young map having great possessions, who asked, What shall I do to be saved? and received the reply: Keep the Commandments.

This broad, general training, which forms and develops human character, must be accomplished to a very considerable degree, before there can be much hope of success in the further stages of spiritual life. First the psychical, and then the spiritual. First the man, then the angel. On this broad, humane and wise foundation does the system of Patanjali rest.

31. The Commandments, not limited to any race, place, time or occasion, universal, are the great obligation.

The Commandments form the broad general training of humanity. Each one of them rests on a universal, spiritual law. Each one of them expresses an attribute or aspect of the Self, the Eternal; when we violate one of the Commandments, we set ourselves against the law and being of the Eternal, thereby bringing ourselves to inevitable con fusion. So the first steps in spiritual life must be taken by bringing ourselves into voluntary obedience to these spiritual laws and thus making ourselves partakers of the spiritual powers, the being of the Eternal Like the law of gravity, the need of air to breathe, these great laws know no exceptions They are in force in all lands, throughout al times, for all mankind.

32. The Rules are these: purity, serenity fervent aspiration, spiritual reading, and per feet obedience to the Master.

Here we have a finer law, one which humanity as a whole is less ready for, less fit to obey. Yet we can see that these Rules are the same in essence as the Commandments, but on a higher, more spiritual plane. The Commandments may be obeyed in outer acts and abstinences; the Rules demand obedience of the heart and spirit, a far more awakened and more positive consciousness. The Rules are the spiritual counterpart of the Commandments, and they have finer degrees, for more advanced spiritual growth.

33. When transgressions hinder, the weight of the imagination should be thrown' on the opposite side.

Let us take a simple case, that of a thief, a habitual criminal, who has drifted into stealing in childhood, before the moral consciousness has awakened. We may imprison such a thief, and deprive him of all possibility of further theft, or of using the divine gift of will. Or we may recognize his disadvantages, and help him gradually to build up possessions which express his will, and draw forth his self-respect. If we imagine that, after he has built well, and his possessions have become dear to him, he himself is robbed, then we can see how he would come vividly to realize the essence of theft and of honesty, and would cleave to honest dealings with firm conviction. In some such way does the great Law teach us. Our sorrows and losses teach us the pain of the sorrow and loss we inflict on others, and so we cease to inflict them.

Now as to the more direct application. To conquer a sin, let heart and mind rest, not on the sin, but on the contrary virtue. Let the sin be forced out by positive growth in the true direction, not by direct opposition. Turn away from the sin and go forward courageously, constructively, creatively, in well-doing. In this way the whole nature will gradually be drawn up to the higher level, on which the sin does not even exist. The conquest of a sin is a matter of growth and evolution, rather than of opposition.

34. Transgressions are injury, falsehood, theft, incontinence, envy; whether committed, or caused, or assented to, through greed, wrath, or infatuation; whether faint, or middling, or excessive; bearing endless, fruit of ignorance and pain. Therefore must the weight be cast on the other side.

Here are the causes of sin: greed, wrath, infatuation, with their effects, ignorance and pain. The causes are to be cured by better wisdom, by a truer understanding of the Self, of Life. For greed cannot endure before the realization that the whole world belongs to the Self, which Self we are; nor can we hold wrath against one who is one with the Self, and therefore with ourselves; nor can infatuation, which is the seeking for the happiness of the All in some limited part of it, survive the knowledge that we are heirs of the All. Therefore let thought and imagination, mind and heart, throw their weight on the other side; the side, not of the world, but of the Self.

35. Where non-injury is perfected, all enmity ceases in the presence of him who possesses it.

We come now to the spiritual powers which result from keeping the Commandments; from the obedience to spiritual law which is the keeping of the Commandments. Where the heart is full of kindness which seeks no injury to another, either in act or thought or wish, this full love creates an atmosphere of harmony, whose benign power touches with healing all who come within its influence. Peace in the heart radiates peace to other hearts, even more surely than contention breeds contention.

36. When he is perfected in truth, all acts and their fruits depend on him.

The commentator thus explains: If he who has attained should say to a man, Become righteous! the man becomes righteous. If he should say, Gain heaven! the man gains heaven. His word is not in vain.

Exactly the same doctrine was taught by the Master who said to his disciples: Receive ye the Holy Ghost: whose soever sins ye remit they are remitted unto them; and whose soever sins ye retain, they are retained.

37. Where cessation from theft is perfected, all treasures present themselves to him who possesses it.

Here is a sentence which may warn us that, beside the outer and apparent meaning, there is in many of these sentences a second and finer significance. The obvious meaning is, that he who has wholly ceased from theft, in act, thought and wish, finds buried treasures in his path, treasures of jewels and gold and pearls. The deeper truth is, that he who in every least thing is wholly honest with the spirit of Life, finds Life supporting him in all things, and gains admittance to the treasure house of Life, the spiritual universe.

38. For him who is perfect in continence, the reward is valour and virility.

The creative power, strong and full of vigour, is no longer dissipated, but turned to spiritual uses. It upholds and endows the spiritual man, conferring on him the creative will, the power to engender spiritual children instead of bodily progeny. An epoch of life, that of man the animal, has come to an end; a new epoch, that of the spiritual man, is opened. The old creative power is superseded and transcended; a new creative power, that of the spiritual man, takes its place, carrying with it the power to work creatively in others for righteousness and eternal life.

One of the commentaries says that he who has attained is able to transfer to the minds of his disciples what he knows concerning divine union, and the means of gaining it. This is one of the powers of purity.

39. Where there is firm conquest of covetousness, he who has conquered it awakes to the how and why of life.

So it is said that, before we can understand the laws of Karma, we must free ourselves from Karma. The conquest of covetousness brings this rich fruit, because the root of covetousness is the desire of the individual soul, the will toward manifested life. And where the desire of the individual soul is overcome by the superb, still life of the universal Soul welling up in the heart within, the great secret is discerned, the secret that the individual soul is not an isolated reality, but the ray, the manifest instrument of the Life, which turns it this way and that until the great work is accomplished, the age-long lesson learned. Thus is the how and why of life disclosed by ceasing from covetousness. The Commentator says that this includes a knowledge of one's former births.

40. Through purity a withdrawal from one's own bodily life, a ceasing from infatuation with the bodily life of others.

As the spiritual light grows in the heart within, as the taste for pure Life grows stronger, the consciousness opens toward the great, secret places within, where all life is one, where all lives are one. Thereafter, this outer, manifested, fugitive life, whether of ourselves or of others, loses something of its charm and glamour, and we seek rather the deep infinitudes.

Instead of the outer form and surroundings of our lives, we long for their inner and everlasting essence. We desire not so much outer converse and closeness to our friends, but rather that quiet communion with them in the inner chamber of the soul, where spirit speaks to spirit, and spirit answers; where alienation and separation never enter; where sickness and sorrow and death cannot come.

41. To the pure of heart come also a quiet spirit, one-pointed thought, the victory over sensuality, and fitness to behold the Soul.

Blessed are the pure in heart, for they shall see God, who is the supreme Soul; the ultimate Self of all beings. In the deepest sense, purity means fitness for this vision, and also a heart cleansed from all disquiet, from all wandering and unbridled thought, from the torment of sensuous imaginings; and when the spirit is thus cleansed and pure, it becomes at one in essence with its source, the great Spirit, the primal Life. One consciousness now thrills through both, for the psychic partition wall is broken down. Then shall the pure in heart see God, because they become God.

42. From acceptance, the disciple gains happiness supreme.

One of the wise has said: accept conditions, accept others, accept yourself. This is the true acceptance, for all these things are what they are through the will of the higher Self, except their deficiencies, which come through thwarting the will of the higher Self, and can be conquered only through compliance with that will. By the true acceptance, the disciple comes into oneness of spirit with the overruling Soul; and, since the own nature of the Soul is being, happiness, bliss, he comes thereby into happiness supreme.

43. The perfection of the powers of the bodily vesture comes through the wearing away of impurities, and through fervent aspiration.

This is true of the physical powers, and of those which dwell in the higher vestures. There must be, first, purity; as the blood must be pure, before one can attain to physical health. But absence of impurity is not in itself enough, else would many nerveless ascetics of the cloisters rank as high saints. There is needed, further, a positive fire of the will; a keen vital vigour for the physical powers, and something finer, purer, stronger, but of kindred essence, for the higher powers. The fire of genius is something more than a phrase, for there can be no genius without the celestial fire of the awakened spiritual will.

44. Through spiritual reading, the disciple gains communion with the divine Power on which his heart is set.

Spiritual reading meant, for ancient India, something more than it does with us. It meant, first, the recital of sacred texts, which, in their very sounds, had mystical potencies; and it meant a recital of texts which were divinely emanated, and held in themselves the living, potent essence of the divine.

For us, spiritual reading means a communing with the recorded teachings of the Masters of wisdom, whereby we read ourselves into the Master's mind, just as through his music one can enter into the mind and soul of the master musician. It has been well said that all true art is contagion of feeling; so that through the true reading of true books we do indeed read ourselves into the spirit of the Masters, share in the atmosphere of their wisdom and power, and come at last into their very presence.

45. Soul-vision is perfected through perfect obedience to the Master.

The sorrow and darkness of life come of the erring personal will which sets itself against the will of the Soul, the one great Life. The error of the personal will is inevitable, since each will must be free to choose, to try and fail, and so to find the path. And sorrow and darkness are inevitable, until the path be found, and the personal will made once more one with the greater Will, wherein it finds rest and power, without losing freedom. In His will is our peace. And with that peace comes light. Soul-vision is perfected through obedience.

46. Right poise must be firm and without strain.

Here we approach a section of the teaching which has manifestly a two-fold meaning. The first is physical, and concerns the bodily position of the student, and the regulation of breathing. These things have their direct influence upon soul-life, the life of the spiritual man, since it is always and everywhere true that our study demands a sound mind in a sound body. The present sentence declares that, for work and for meditation, the position of the body must be steady and without strain, in order that the finer currents of life may run their course.

It applies further to the poise of the soul, that fine balance and stability which nothing can shake, where the consciousness rests on the firm foundation of spiritual being. This is indeed the house set upon a rock, which the winds and waves beat upon in vain.

47. Right poise is to be gained by steady and temperate effort, and by setting the heart upon the everlasting.

Here again, there is the two-fold meaning, for physical poise is to be gained by steady effort of the muscles, by gradual and wise training, linked with a right understanding of, and relation with, the universal force of gravity. Uprightness of body demands that both these conditions shall be fulfilled.

In like manner the firm and upright poise of the spiritual man is to be gained by steady and continued effort, always guided by wisdom, and by setting the heart on the Eternal, filling the soul with the atmosphere of the spiritual world. Neither is effective without the other. Aspiration without effort brings weakness; effort without aspiration brings a false strength, not resting on enduring things. The two together make for the right poise which sets the spiritual man firmly and steadfastly on his feet.

48. The fruit of right poise is the strength to resist the shocks of infatuation or sorrow.

In the simpler physical sense, which is also coveted by the wording of the original, this sentence means that wise effort establishes such bodily poise that the accidents of life cannot disturb it, as the captain remains steady, though disaster overtake his ship.

But the deeper sense is far more important. The spiritual man, too, must learn to withstand all shocks, to remain steadfast through the perturbations of external things and the storms and whirlwinds of the psychical world. This is the power which is gained by wise, continuous effort, and by filling the spirit with the atmosphere of the Eternal.

49. When this is gained, there follows the right guidance of the life-currents, the control of the incoming and outgoing breath.

It is well understood to-day that most of our maladies come from impure conditions of the blood. It is coming to be understood that right breathing, right oxygenation, will do very much to keep the blood clean and pure. Therefore a right knowledge of breathing is a part of the science of life.

But the deeper meaning is, that the spiritual man, when he has gained poise through right effort and aspiration, can stand firm, and guide the currents of his life, both the incoming current of events, and the outgoing current of his acts.

Exactly the same symbolism is used in the saying: Not that which goeth into the mouth defileth a man; but that which cometh out of the mouth, this defileth a man.... Those things which proceed out of the mouth come forth from the heart ... out of the heart proceed evil thoughts, murders, uncleanness, thefts, false witness, blasphemies. Therefore the first step in purification is to keep the Commandments.

50. The life-current is either outward, or inward, or balanced; it is regulated according to place, time, number; it is prolonged and subtle.

The technical, physical side of this has its value. In the breath, there should be right inbreathing, followed by the period of pause, when the air comes into contact with the blood, and this again followed by right outbreathing, even, steady, silent. Further, the lungs should be evenly filled; many maladies may arise from the neglect and consequent weakening of some region of the lungs. And the number of breaths is so important, so closely related to health, that every nurse's chart records it.

But the deeper meaning is concerned with the currents of life; with that which goeth into and cometh out of the heart.

51. The fourth degree transcends external and internal objects.

The inner meaning seems to be that, in addition to the three degrees of control already described, control, that is, over the incoming current of life, over the outgoing current, and over the condition of pause or quiesence, there is a fourth degree of control, which holds in complete mastery both the outer passage of events and the inner currents of thoughts and emotions; a condition of perfect poise and stability in the midst of the flux of things outward and inward.

52. Thereby is worn away the veil which covers up the light.

The veil is the psychic nature, the web of emotions, desires, argumentative trains of thought, which cover up and obscure the truth by absorbing the entire attention and keeping the consciousness in the psychic realm. When hopes and fears are reckoned at their true worth, in comparison with lasting possessions of the Soul; when the outer reflections of things have ceased to distract us from inner realities; when argumentative-thought no longer entangles us, but yields its place to flashing intuition, the certainty which springs from within; then is the veil worn away, the consciousness is drawn from the psychical to the spiritual, from the temporal to the Eternal. Then is the light unveiled.

53. Thence comes the mind's power to hold itself in the light.

It has been well said, that what we most need is the faculty of spiritual attention; and in the same direction of thought it has been eloquently declared that prayer does not consist in our catching God's attention, but rather in our allowing God to hold our attention.

The vital matter is, that we need to disentangle our consciousness from the noisy and perturbed thraldom of the psychical, and to come to consciousness as the spiritual man. This we must do, first, by purification, through the Commandments and the Rules; and, second, through the faculty of spiritual attention, by steadily heeding endless fine intimations of the spiritual power within us, and by intending our consciousness thereto; thus by degrees transferring the centre of consciousness from the psychical to the spiritual. It is a question, first, of love, and then of attention.

54. The right Withdrawal is the disengaging of the powers from entanglement in outer things, as the psychic nature has been withdrawn and stilled.

To understand this, let us reverse the process, and think of the one consciousness, centred in the Soul, gradually expanding and taking on the form of the different perceptive powers; the one will, at the same time, differentiating itself into the varied powers of action.

Now let us imagine this to be reversed, so that the spiritual force, which has gone into the differentiated powers, is once more gathered together into the inner power of intuition and spiritual will, taking on that unity which is the hall-mark of spiritual things, as diversity is the seal of material things.

It is all a matter of love for the quality of spiritual consciousness, as against psychical consciousness, of love and attention. For where the heart is, there will the treasure be also; where the consciousness is, there will the vesture with its powers be developed.

55. Thereupon follows perfect mastery over the powers.

When the spiritual condition which we have described is reached, with its purity, poise, and illuminated vision, the spiritual man is coming into his inheritance, and gaining complete mastery of his powers.

Indeed, much of the struggle to keep the Commandments and the Rules has been paving the way for this mastery; through this very struggle and sacrifice the mastery has become possible; just as, to use St. Paul's simile, the athlete gains the mastery in the contest and the race through the sacrifice of his long and arduous training. Thus he gains the crown.

INTRODUCTION TO BOOK III

The third book of the Sutras is the Book of Spiritual Powers. In considering these spiritual powers, two things must be understood and kept in memory. The first of these is this: These spiritual powers can only be gained when the development described in the first and second books has been measurably attained; when the Commandments have been kept, the Rules faithfully followed, and the experiences which are described have been passed through. For only after this is the spiritual man so far grown, so far disentangled from the psychical bandages and veils which have confined and blinded him, that he can use his proper powers and faculties. For this is the secret of all spiritual powers: they are in no sense an abnormal or supernatural overgrowth upon the material man, but are rather the powers and faculties inherent in the spiritual man, entirely natural to him, and coming naturally into activity, as the spiritual man is disentangled and liberated from psychical bondage, through keeping the Commandments and Rules already set forth.

As the personal man is the limitation and inversion of the spiritual man, all his faculties and powers are inversions of the powers of the spiritual man. In a single phrase, his self seeking is the inversion of the Self-seeking which is the very being of the spiritual man: the ceaseless search after the divine and august Self of all beings. This inversion is corrected by keeping the Commandments and Rules, and gradually, as the inversion is overcome, the spiritual man is extricated, and comes into possession and free exercise of his powers. The spiritual powers, therefore, are the powers of the grown and liberated spiritual man. They can only be developed and used as the spiritual man grows and attains liberation through obedience. This is the first thing to be kept in mind, in all that is said of spiritual powers in the third and fourth books of the Sutras. The second thing to be understood and kept in mind is this:

Just as our modern sages have discerned and taught that all matter is ultimately one and eternal, definitely related throughout the whole wide universe; just as they have discerned and taught that all force is one and eternal, so coordinated throughout the whole universe that whatever affects any atom measurably affects the whole boundless realm of matter and force, to the most distant star or nebula on the dim confines of space; so the ancient sages had discerned and taught that all consciousness is one, immortal, indivisible, infinite; so finely correlated and continuous that whatever is perceived by any consciousness is, whether actually or potentially, within the reach of all consciousness, and therefore within the reach of any consciousness. This has been well expressed by saying that all souls are fundamentally one with the Oversoul; that the Son of God, and all Sons of God, are fundamentally one with the Father. When the consciousness is cleared of psychic bonds and veils, when the spiritual man is able to stand, to see, then this superb law comes into effect: whatever is within the knowledge of any consciousness, and this includes the whole infinite universe, is within his reach, and may, if he wills, be made a part of his consciousness. This he may attain through his fundamental unity with the Oversoul, by raising himself toward the consciousness above him, and drawing on its resources. The Son, if he would work miracles, whether of perception or of action, must come often into the presence of the Father. This is the birthright of the spiritual man; through it he comes into possession of his splendid and immortal powers. Let it be clearly kept in mind that what is here to be related of the spiritual man, and his exalted powers, must in no wise be detached from what has gone before. The being, the very inception, of the spiritual man depends on the purification and moral attainment already detailed, and can in no wise dispense with these or curtail them.

Let no one imagine that the true life, the true powers of the spiritual man, can be attained by any way except the hard way of sacrifice, of trial, of renunciation, of selfless self-conquest and genuine devotion to the weal of all others. Only thus can the golden gates be reached and entered. Only thus can we attain to that pure world wherein the spiritual man lives, and moves, and has his being. Nothing impure, nothing unholy can ever cross that threshold, least of all impure motives or self seeking desires. These must be burnt away before an entrance to that world can be gained.

But where there is light, there is shadow; and the lofty light of the soul casts upon the clouds of the mid-world the shadow of the spiritual man and of his powers; the bastard vesture and the bastard powers of psychism are easily attained; yet, even when attained, they are a delusion, the very essence of unreality.

Therefore ponder well the earlier rules, and lay a firm foundation of courage, sacrifice, selflessness, holiness.

BOOK III

1. The binding of the perceiving consciousness to a certain region is attention (dharana).

Emerson quotes Sir Isaac Newton as saying that he made his great discoveries by intending his mind on them. That is what is meant here. I read the page of a book while inking of something else. At the end of he page, I have no idea of what it is about, and read it again, still thinking of something else, with the same result. Then I wake up, so to speak, make an effort of attention, fix my thought on what I am reading, and easily take in its meaning. The act of will, the effort of attention, the intending of the mind on each word and line of the page, just as the eyes are focussed on each word and line, is the power here contemplated. It is the power to focus the consciousness on a given spot, and hold it there Attention is the first and indispensable step in all knowledge. Attention to spiritual things is the first step to spiritual knowledge.

2. A prolonged holding of the perceiving consciousness in that region is meditation (dhyana).

This will apply equally to outer and inner things. I may for a moment fix my attention on some visible object, in a single penetrating glance, or I may hold the attention fixedly on it until it reveals far more of its nature than a single glance could perceive. The first is the focussing of the searchlight of consciousness upon the object. The other is the holding of the white beam of light steadily and persistently on the object, until it yields up the secret of its details. So for things within; one may fix the inner glance for a moment on spiritual things, or one may hold the consciousness steadily upon them, until what was in the dark slowly comes forth into the light, and yields up its immortal secret. But this is possible only for the spiritual man, after the Commandments and the Rules have been kept; for until this is done, the thronging storms of psychical thoughts dissipate and distract the attention, so that it will not remain fixed on spiritual things. The cares of this world, the deceitfulness of riches, choke the word of the spiritual message.

3. When the perceiving consciousness in this meditative is wholly given to illuminating the essential meaning of the object contemplated, and is freed from the sense of separateness and personality, this is contemplation (samadhi).

Let us review the steps so far taken. First, the beam of perceiving consciousness is focussed on a certain region or subject, through the effort of attention. Then this attending consciousness is held on its object. Third, there is the ardent will to know its meaning, to illumine it with comprehending thought. Fourth, all personal bias—all desire merely to indorse a previous opinion and so prove oneself right, and all desire for personal profit or gratification must be quite put away. There must be a purely disinterested love of truth for its own sake. Thus is the perceiving consciousness made void, as it were, of all personality or sense of separateness. The personal limitation stands aside and lets the All-consciousness come to bear upon the problem. The Oversoul bends its ray upon the object, and illumines it with pure light.

4. When these three, Attention, Meditation Contemplation, are exercised at once, this is perfectly concentrated Meditation (sanyama).

When the personal limitation of the perceiving consciousness stands aside, and allows the All-conscious to come to bear upon the problem, then arises that real knowledge which is called a flash of genius; that real knowledge which makes discoveries, and without which no discovery can be made, however painstaking the effort. For genius is the vision of the spiritual man, and that vision is a question of growth rather than present effort; though right effort, rightly continued, will in time infallibly lead to growth and vision. Through the power thus to set aside personal limitation, to push aside petty concerns and cares, and steady the whole nature and will in an ardent love of truth and desire to know it; through the power thus to make way for the All-consciousness, all great men make their discoveries. Newton, watching the apple fall to the earth, was able to look beyond, to see the subtle waves of force pulsating through apples and worlds and suns and galaxies, and thus to perceive universal gravitation. The Oversoul, looking through his eyes, recognized the universal force, one of its own children. Darwin, watching the forms and motions of plants and animals, let the same august consciousness come to bear on them, and saw infinite growth perfected through ceaseless struggle. He perceived the superb process of evolution, the Oversoul once more recognizing its own. Fraunhofer, noting the dark lines in the band of sunlight in his spectroscope, divined their identity with the bright lines in the spectra of incandescent iron, sodium and the rest, and so saw the oneness of substance in the worlds and suns, the unity of the materials of the universe. Once again the Oversoul, looking with his eyes, recognized its own. So it is with all true knowledge. But the mind must transcend its limitations, its idiosyncrasies; there must be purity, for to the pure in heart is the promise, that they shall see God.

5. By mastering this perfectly concentrated Meditation, there comes the illumination of perception.

The meaning of this is illustrated by what has been said before. When the spiritual man is able to throw aside the trammels of emotional and mental limitation, and to open his eyes, he sees clearly, he attains to illuminated perception. A poet once said that Occultism is the conscious cultivation of genius; and it is certain that the awakened spiritual man attains to the perceptions of genius. Genius is the vision, the power, of the spiritual man, whether its possessor recognizes this or not. All true knowledge is of the spiritual man. The greatest in all ages have recognized this and put their testimony on record. The great in wisdom who have not consciously recognized it, have ever been full of the spirit of reverence, of selfless devotion to truth, of humility, as was Darwin; and reverence and humility are the unconscious recognition of the nearness of the Spirit, that Divinity which broods over us, a Master o'er a slave.

6. This power is distributed in ascending degrees.

It is to be attained step by step. It is a question, not of miracle, but of evolution, of growth. Newton had to master the multiplication table, then the four rules of arithmetic, then the rudiments of algebra, before he came to the binomial theorem. At each point, there was attention, concentration, insight; until these were attained, no progress to the next point was possible. So with Darwin. He had to learn the form and use of leaf and flower, of bone and muscle; the characteristics of genera and species; the distribution of plants and animals, before he had in mind that nexus of knowledge on which the light of his great idea was at last able to shine. So is it with all knowledge. So is it with spiritual knowledge. Take the matter this way: The first subject for the exercise of my spiritual insight is my day, with its circumstances, its hindrances, its opportunities, its duties. I do what I can to solve it, to fulfil its duties, to learn its lessons. I try to live my day with aspiration and faith. That is the first step. By doing this, I gather a harvest for the evening, I gain a deeper insight into life, in virtue of which I begin the next day with a certain advantage, a certain spiritual advance and attainment. So with all successive days. In faith and aspiration, we pass from day to day, in growing knowledge and power, with never more than one day to solve at a time, until all life becomes radiant and transparent.

7. This threefold power, of Attention, Meditation, Contemplation, is more interior than the means of growth previously described.

Very naturally so; because the means of growth previously described were concerned with the extrication of the spiritual man from psychic bondages and veils; while this threefold power is to be exercised by the spiritual man thus extricated and standing on his feet, viewing life with open eyes.

8. But this triad is still exterior to the soul vision which is unconditioned, free from the seed of mental analyses.

The reason is this: The threefold power we have been considering, the triad of Attention, Contemplation, Meditation is, so far as we have yet considered it, the focussing of the beam of perceiving consciousness upon some form of manifesting being, with a view of understanding it completely. There is a higher stage, where the beam of consciousness is turned back upon itself, and the individual consciousness enters into, and knows, the All consciousness. This is a being, a being in immortality, rather than a knowing; it is free from mental analysis or mental forms. It is not an activity of the higher mind, even the mind of the spiritual man. It is an activity of the soul. Had Newton risen to this higher stage, he would have known, not the laws of motion, but that high Being, from whose Life comes eternal motion. Had Darwin risen to this, he would have seen the Soul, whose graduated thought and being all evolution expresses. There are, therefore, these two perceptions: that of living things, and that of the Life; that of the Soul's works, and that of the Soul itself.

9. One of the ascending degrees is the development of Control. First there is the overcoming of the mind-impress of excitation. Then comes the manifestation of the mind-impress of Control. Then the perceiving consciousness follows after the moment of Control.

This is the development of Control. The meaning seems to be this: Some object enters the field of observation, and at first violently excites the mind, stirring up curiosity, fear, wonder; then the consciousness returns upon itself, as it were, and takes the perception firmly in hand, steadying itself, and viewing the matter calmly from above. This steadying effort of the will upon the perceiving consciousness is Control, and immediately upon it follows perception, understanding, insight.

Take a trite example. Supposing one is walking in an Indian forest. A charging elephant suddenly appears. The man is excited by astonishment, and, perhaps, terror. But he exercises an effort of will, perceives the situation in its true bearings, and recognizes that a certain thing must be done; in this case, probably, that he must get out of the way as quickly as possible.

Or a comet, unheralded, appears in the sky like a flaming sword. The beholder is at first astonished, perhaps terror-stricken; but he takes himself in hand, controls his thoughts, views the apparition calmly, and finally calculates its orbit and its relation to meteor showers.

These are extreme illustrations; but with all knowledge the order of perception is the same: first, the excitation of the mind by the new object impressed on it; then the control of the mind from within; upon which follows the perception of the nature of the object. Where the eyes of the spiritual man are open, this will be a true and penetrating spiritual perception. In some such way do our living experiences come to us; first, with a shock of pain; then the Soul steadies itself and controls the pain; then the spirit perceives the lesson of the event, and its bearing upon the progressive revelation of life.

10. Through frequent repetition of this process, the mind becomes habituated to it, and there arises an equable flow of perceiving consciousness.

Control of the mind by the Soul, like control of the muscles by the mind, comes by practice, and constant voluntary repetition.

As an example of control of the muscles by the mind, take the ceaseless practice by which a musician gains mastery over his instrument, or a fencer gains skill with a rapier. Innumerable small efforts of attention will make a result which seems well-nigh miraculous; which, for the novice, is really miraculous. Then consider that far more wonderful instrument, the perceiving mind, played on by that fine musician, the Soul. Here again, innumerable small efforts of attention will accumulate into mastery, and a mastery worth winning. For a concrete example, take the gradual conquest of each day, the effort to live that day for the Soul. To him that is faithful unto death, the Master gives the crown of life.

11. The gradual conquest of the mind's tendency to flit from one object to another, and the power of one-pointedness, make the development of Contemplation.

As an illustration of the mind's tendency to flit from one object to another, take a small boy, learning arithmetic. He begins: two ones are two; three ones are three-and then he thinks of three coins in his pocket, which will purchase so much candy, in the store down the street, next to the toy-shop, where are base-balls, marbles and so on,—and then he comes back with a jerk, to four ones are four. So with us also. We are seeking the meaning of our task, but the mind takes advantage of a moment of slackened attention, and flits off from one frivolous detail to another, till we suddenly come back to consciousness after traversing leagues of space. We must learn to conquer this, and to go back within ourselves into the beam of perceiving consciousness itself, which is a beam of the Oversoul. This is the true onepointedness, the bringing of our consciousness to a focus in the Soul.

12. When, following this, the controlled manifold tendency and the aroused one-pointedness are equally balanced parts of the perceiving consciousness, his the development of one-pointedness.

This would seem to mean that the insight which is called one-pointedness has two sides, equally balanced. There is, first, the manifold aspect of any object, the sum of all its characteristics and properties. This is to be held firmly in the mind. Then there is the perception of the object as a unity, as a whole, the perception of its essence. First, the details must be clearly perceived; then the essence must be comprehended. When the two processes are equally balanced, the true onepointedness is attained. Everything has these two sides, the side of difference and the side of unity; there is the individual and there is the genus; the pole of matter and diversity, and the pole of oneness and spirit. To see the object truly, we must see both.

13. Through this, the inherent character, distinctive marks and conditions of being and powers, according to their development, are made clear.

By the power defined in the preceding sutra, the inherent character, distinctive marks and conditions of beings and powers are made clear. For through this power, as defined, we get a twofold view of each object, seeing at once all its individual characteristics and its essential character, species and genus; we see it in relation to itself, and in relation to the Eternal. Thus we see a rose as that particular flower, with its colour and scent, its peculiar fold of each petal; but we also see in it the species, the family to which it belongs, with its relation to all plants, to all life, to Life itself. So in any day, we see events and circumstances; we also see in it the lesson set for the soul by the Eternal.

14. Every object has its characteristics which are already quiescent, those which are active, and those which are not yet definable.

Every object has characteristics belonging to its past, its present and its future. In a fir tree, for example, there are the stumps or scars of dead branches, which once represented its foremost growth; there are the branches with their needles spread out to the air; there are the buds at the end of each branch and twig, which carry the still closely packed needles which are the promise of the future. In like manner, the chrysalis has, as its past, the caterpillar; as its future, the butterfly. The man has, in his past, the animal; in his future, the angel. Both are visible even now in his face. So with all things, for all things change and grow.

15. Difference in stage is the cause of difference in development.

This but amplifies what has just been said. The first stage is the sapling, the caterpillar, the animal. The second stage is the growing tree, the chrysalis, the man. The third is the splendid pine, the butterfly, the angel. Difference of stage is the cause of difference of development. So it is among men, and among the races of men.

16. Through perfectly concentrated Meditation on the three stages of development comes a knowledge of past and future.

We have taken our illustrations from natural science, because, since every true discovery in natural science is a divination of a law in nature, attained through a flash of genius, such discoveries really represent acts of spiritual perception, acts of perception by the spiritual man, even though they are generally not so recognized. So we may once more use the same illustration. Perfectly concentrated Meditation, perfect insight into the chrysalis, reveals the caterpillar that it has been, the butterfly that it is destined to be. He who knows the seed, knows the seed-pod or ear it has come from, and the plant that is to come from it. So in like manner he who really knows today, and the heart of to-day, knows its parent yesterday and its child tomorrow. Past, present and future are all in the Eternal. He who dwells in the Eternal knows all three.

17. The sound and the object and the thought called up by a word are confounded because they are all blurred together in the mind. By perfectly concentrated Meditation on the distinction between them, there comes an understanding of the sounds uttered by all beings.

It must be remembered that we are speaking of perception by the spiritual man.

Sound, like every force, is the expression of a power of the Eternal. Infinite shades of this power are expressed in the infinitely varied tones of sound. He who, having entry to the consciousness of the Eternal knows the essence of this power, can divine the meanings of all sounds, from the voice of the insect to the music of the spheres.

In like manner, he who has attained to spiritual vision can perceive the mind-images in the thoughts of others, with the shade of feeling which goes with them, thus reading their thoughts as easily as he hears their words. Every one has the germ of this power, since difference of tone will give widely differing meanings to the same words, meanings which are intuitively perceived by everyone.

18. When the mind-impressions become visible, there comes an understanding of previous births.

This is simple enough if we grasp the truth of rebirth. The fine harvest of past experiences is drawn into the spiritual nature, forming, indeed, the basis of its development. When the consciousness has been raised to a point above these fine subjective impressions, and can look down upon them from above, this will in itself be a remembering of past births.

19. By perfectly concentrated Meditation on mind-images is gained the understanding of the thoughts of others.

Here, for those who can profit by it, is the secret of thought-reading. Take the simplest case of intentional thought transference. It is the testimony of those who have done this, that the perceiving mind must be stilled, before the mind-image projected by the other mind can be seen. With it comes a sense of the feeling and temper of the other mind and so on, in higher degrees.

20. But since that on which the thought in the mind of another rests is not objective to the thought-reader's consciousness, he perceives the thought only, and not also that on which the thought rests.

The meaning appears to be simple: One may be able to perceive the thoughts of some one at a distance; one cannot, by that means alone, also perceive the external surroundings of that person, which arouse these thoughts.

21. By perfectly concentrated Meditation on the form of the body, by arresting the body's perceptibility, and by inhibiting the eye's power of sight, there comes the power to make the body invisible.

There are many instances of the exercise of this power, by mesmerists, hypnotists and the like; and we may simply call it an instance of the power of suggestion. Shankara tells us that by this power the popular magicians of the East perform their wonders, working on the mind-images of others, while remaining invisible themselves. It is all a question of being able to see and control the mind-images.

22. The works which fill out the life-span may be either immediately or gradually operative. By perfectly

concentrated Meditation on these comes a knowledge of the time of the end, as also through signs.

A garment which is wet, says the commentator, may be hung up to dry, and so dry rapidly, or it may be rolled in a ball and dry slowly; so a fire may blaze or smoulder. Thus it is with Karma, the works that fill out the life-span. By an insight into the mental forms and forces which make up Karma, there comes a knowledge of the rapidity or slowness of their development, and of the time when the debt will be paid.

23. By perfectly concentrated Meditation on sympathy, compassion and kindness, is gained the power of interior union with others.

Unity is the reality; separateness the illusion. The nearer we come to reality, the nearer we come to unity of heart. Sympathy, compassion, kindness are modes of this unity of heart, whereby we rejoice with those who rejoice, and weep with those who weep. These things are learned by desiring to learn them.

24. By perfectly concentrated Meditation on power, even such power as that of the elephant may be gained.

This is a pretty image. Elephants possess not only force, but poise and fineness of control. They can lift a straw, a child, a tree with perfectly judged control and effort. So the simile is a good one. By detachment, by withdrawing into the soul's reservoir of power, we can gain all these, force and fineness and poise; the ability to handle with equal mastery things small and great, concrete and abstract alike.

25. By bending upon them the awakened inner light, there comes a knowledge of things subtle, or concealed, or obscure.

As was said at the outset, each consciousness is related to all consciousness; and, through it, has a potential consciousness of all things; whether subtle or concealed or obscure. An understanding of this great truth will come with practice. As one of the wise has said, we have no conception of the power of Meditation.

26. By perfectly concentrated Meditation on the sun comes a knowledge of the worlds.

This has several meanings: First, by a knowledge of the constitution of the sun, astronomers can understand the kindred nature of the stars. And it is said that there is a finer astronomy, where the spiritual man is the astronomer. But the sun also means the Soul, and through knowledge of the Soul comes a knowledge of the realms of life.

27. By perfectly concentrated Meditation on the moon comes a knowledge of the lunar mansions.

Here again are different meanings. The moon is, first, the companion planet, which, each day, passes backward through one mansion of the stars. By watching the moon, the boundaries of the mansion are learned, with their succession in the great time-dial of the sky. But the moon also symbolizes the analytic mind, with its divided realms; and these, too, may be understood through perfectly concentrated Meditation.

28. By perfectly concentrated Meditation on the fixed pole-star comes a knowledge of the motions of the stars.

Addressing Duty, stern daughter of the Voice of God, Wordsworth finely said:

Thou cost preserve the stars from wrong,
And the most ancient heavens through thee are fresh and strong—

thus suggesting a profound relation between the moral powers and the powers that rule the worlds. So in this Sutra the fixed polestar is the eternal spirit about which all things move, as well as the star toward which points the axis of the earth. Deep mysteries attend both, and the veil of mystery is only to be raised by Meditation, by open-eyed vision of the awakened spiritual man.

29. Perfectly concentrated Meditation on the centre of force in the lower trunk brings an understanding of the order of the bodily powers.

We are coming to a vitally important part of the teaching of Yoga: namely, the spiritual man's attainment of full self-consciousness, the awakening of the spiritual man as a self-conscious individual, behind and above the natural man. In this awakening, and in the process of gestation which precedes it, there is a close relation with the powers of the natural man, which are, in a certain sense, the projection, outward and downward, of the powers of the spiritual man. This is notably true of that creative power of the spiritual man which, when embodied in the natural man, becomes the power of generation. Not only is this power the cause of the continuance of the bodily race of mankind, but further, in the individual, it is the key to the dominance of the personal life. Rising, as it were, through the life-channels of the body, it flushes the personality with physical force, and maintains and colours the illusion that the physical life is the dominant and all-important expression of life. In due time, when the spiritual man has begun to take form, the creative force will be drawn off, and become operative in building the body of the spiritual man, just as it has been operative in the building of physical bodies, through generation in the natural world.

Perfectly concentrated Meditation on the nature of this force means, first, that rising of the consciousness into the spiritual world, already described, which gives the one sure foothold for Meditation; and then, from that spiritual point of vantage, not only an insight into the creative force, in its spiritual and physical aspects, but also a gradually attained control of this wonderful force, which will mean its direction to the body of the spiritual man, and its gradual withdrawal from the body of the natural man, until the over-pressure, so general and such a fruitful source of misery in our day, is abated, and purity takes the place of passion. This over pressure, which is the cause of so many evils and so much of human shame, is an abnormal, not a natural, condition. It is primarily due to spiritual blindness, to blindness regarding the spiritual man, and ignorance even of his existence; for by this blind ignorance are closed the channels through which, were they open, the creative force could flow into the body of the spiritual man, there building up an immortal vesture. There is no cure for blindness, with its consequent over-pressure and attendant misery and shame, but spiritual vision, spiritual aspiration, sacrifice, the new birth from above. There is no other way to lighten the burden, to lift the misery and shame from human life. Therefore, let us follow after sacrifice and aspiration, let us seek the light. In this way only shall we gain that insight into the order of the bodily powers, and that mastery of them, which this Sutra implies.

30. By perfectly concentrated Meditation on the centre of force in the well of the throat, there comes the cessation of hunger and thirst.

We are continuing the study of the bodily powers and centres of force in their relation to the powers and forces of the spiritual man. We have already considered the dominant power of physical life, the creative power which secures the continuance of physical life; and, further, the manner in which, through aspiration and sacrifice, it is gradually raised and set to the work of upbuilding the body of the spiritual man. We come now to the dominant psychic force, the power which manifests itself in speech, and in virtue of which the voice may carry so much of the personal magnetism, endowing the orator with a tongue of fire, magical in its power to arouse and rule the emotions of his hearers. This emotional power, this distinctively psychical force, is the cause of "hunger and thirst," the psychical hunger and thirst for sensations, which is the source of our two-sided life of emotionalism, with its hopes and fears, its expectations and memories, its desires and hates. The source of this psychical power, or, perhaps we should say, its centre of activity in the physical body is said to be in the cavity of the throat. Thus, in the Taittiriya Upanishad it is written: "There is this shining ether in the inner being. Therein is the spiritual man, formed through thought, immortal, golden. Inward, in the palate, the organ that hangs down like a nipple,-this is the womb of Indra. And there, where the dividing of the hair turns, extending upward to the crown of the head."

Indra is the name given to the creative power of which we have spoken, and which, we are told, resides in "the organ which hangs down like a nipple, inward, in the palate."

31. By perfectly concentrated Meditation on the centre of force in the channel called the "tortoise-formed," comes steadfastness.

We are concerned now with the centre of nervous or psychical force below the cavity of the throat, in the chest, in which is felt the sensation of fear; the centre, the disturbance of which sets the heart beating miserably with dread, or which produces that sense of terror through which the heart is said to stand still.

When the truth concerning fear is thoroughly mastered, through spiritual insight into the immortal, fearless life, then this force is perfectly controlled; there is no more fear, just as, through the control of the psychic power which works through the nerve-centre in the throat, there comes a cessation of "hunger and thirst." Thereafter, these forces, or their spiritual prototypes, are turned to the building of the spiritual man.

Always, it must be remembered, the victory is first a spiritual one; only later does it bring control of the bodily powers.

32. Through perfectly concentrated Meditation on the light in the head comes the vision of the Masters who have attained.

The tradition is, that there is a certain centre of force in the head, perhaps the "pineal gland," which some of our Western philosophers have supposed to be the dwelling of the soul, a centre which is, as it were, the door way between the natural and the spiritual man. It is the seat of that better and wiser consciousness behind the outward looking consciousness in the forward part of the head; that better and wiser consciousness of "the back of the mind," which views spiritual things, and seeks to impress the spiritual view on the outward looking consciousness in the forward part of the head. It is the spiritual man seeking to guide the natural man, seeking to bring the natural man to concern himself with the things of his immortality. This is suggested in the words of the Upanishad already quoted: "There, where the dividing of the hair turns, extending upward to the crown of the head"; all of which may sound very fantastical, until one comes to understand it.

It is said that when this power is fully awakened, it brings a vision of the great Companions of the spiritual man, those who have already attained, crossing over to the further shore of the sea of death and rebirth. Perhaps it is to this divine sight that the Master alluded, who is reported to have said: "I counsel you to buy of me eye-salve, that you may see." It is of this same vision of the great Companions, the children of light, that a seer wrote:

"Though inland far we be,
Our souls have sight of that immortal sea
Which brought us hither,
Can in a moment travel thither,
And see the Children sport upon the shore
And hear the mighty waters rolling evermore."

33. Or through the divining power of tuition he knows all things.

This is really the supplement, the spiritual side, of the Sutra just translated. Step by step, as the better consciousness, the spiritual view, gains force in the back of the mind, so, in the same measure, the spiritual man is gaining the power to see: learning to open the spiritual eyes. When the eyes are fully opened, the spiritual man beholds the great Companions standing about him; he has begun to "know all things."

This divining power of intuition is the power which lies above and behind the so-called rational mind; the rational mind formulates a question and lays it before the intuition, which gives a real answer, often immediately distorted by the rational mind, yet always embodying a kernel of truth. It is by this process, through which the rational mind brings questions to the intuition for solution, that the truths of science are reached, the flashes of discovery and genius. But this higher power need not work in subordination to the so-called rational mind, it may act directly, as full illumination, "the vision and the faculty divine."

34 By perfectly concentrated Meditation on the heart, the interior being, comes the knowledge of consciousness.

The heart here seems to mean, as it so often does in the Upanishads, the interior, spiritual nature, the consciousness of the spiritual man, which is related to the heart, and to the wisdom of the heart. By steadily seeking after, and finding, the consciousness of the spiritual man, by coming to consciousness as the spiritual man, a perfect knowledge of consciousness will be attained. For the consciousness of the spiritual man has this divine quality: while being and remaining a truly individual consciousness, it at the same time flows over, as it were, and blends with the Divine Consciousness above and about it, the consciousness of the great Companions; and by showing itself to be one with the Divine Consciousness, it reveals the nature of all consciousness, the secret that all consciousness is One and Divine.

35. The personal self seeks to feast on life, through a failure to perceive the distinction between the personal self and the spiritual man. All personal experience really exists for the sake of another: namely, the spiritual man. By perfectly concentrated Meditation on experience for the sake of the Self, comes a knowledge of the spiritual man.

The divine ray of the Higher Self, which is eternal, impersonal and abstract, descends into life, and forms a personality, which, through the stress and storm of life, is hammered into a definite and concrete self-conscious individuality. The problem is, to blend these two powers, taking the eternal and spiritual being of the first, and blending with it, transferring into it, the self-conscious individuality of the second; and thus bringing to life a third being, the spiritual man, who is heir to the immortality of his father, the Higher Self, and yet has the self-conscious, concrete individuality of his other parent, the personal self. This is the true immaculate conception, the new birth from above, "conceived of the Holy Spirit." Of this new birth it is said: "that which is born of the Spirit is spirit: ye must be born again."

Rightly understood, therefore, the whole life of the personal man is for another, not for himself. He exists only to render his very life and all his experience for the building up of the spiritual man. Only through failure to see this, does he seek enjoyment for himself, seek to secure the feasts of life for himself; not understanding that he must live for the other, live sacrificially, offering both feasts and his very being on the altar; giving himself as a contribution for the building of the spiritual man. When he does understand this, and lives for the Higher Self, setting his heart and thought on the Higher Self, then his sacrifice bears divine fruit, the spiritual man is built up, consciousness awakes in him, and he comes fully into being as a divine and immortal individuality.

36. Thereupon are born the divine power of intuition, and the hearing, the touch, the vision, the taste and the power of smell of the spiritual man.

When, in virtue of the perpetual sacrifice of the personal man, daily and hourly giving his life for his divine brother the spiritual man, and through the radiance ever pouring down from the Higher Self, eternal in the Heavens, the spiritual man comes to birth,-there awake in him those powers whose physical counterparts we know in the personal man. The spiritual man begins to see, to hear, to touch, to taste. And, besides the senses of the spiritual man, there awakes his mind, that divine counterpart of the mind of the physical man, the power of direct and immediate knowledge, the power of spiritual intuition, of divination. This power, as we have seen, owes its virtue to the unity, the continuity, of consciousness, whereby whatever is known to any consciousness, is knowable by any other consciousness. Thus the consciousness of the spiritual man, who lives above our narrow barriers of separateness, is in intimate touch with the consciousness of the great Companions, and can draw on that vast reservoir for all real needs. Thus arises within the spiritual man that certain knowledge which is called intuition, divination, illumination.

37. These powers stand in contradistinction to the highest spiritual vision. In manifestation they are called magical powers.

The divine man is destined to supersede the spiritual man, as the spiritual man supersedes the natural man. Then the disciple becomes a Master. The opened powers of tile spiritual man, spiritual vision, hearing, and touch, stand, therefore, in contradistinction to the higher divine power above them, and must in no wise be regarded as the end of the way, for the path has no end, but rises ever to higher and higher glories; the soul's growth and splendour have no limit. So that, if the spiritual powers we have been considering are regarded as in any sense final, they are a hindrance, a barrier to the far higher powers of the divine man. But viewed from below, from the standpoint of normal physical experience, they are powers truly magical; as the powers natural to a four-dimensional being will appear magical to a three-dimensional being.

38. Through the weakening of the causes of bondage, and by learning the method of sassing, the consciousness is transferred to the other body.

In due time, after the spiritual man has been formed and grown stable through the forces and virtues already enumerated, and after the senses of the spiritual man have awaked, there comes the transfer of the dominant consciousness, the sense of individuality, from the physical to the spiritual man. Thereafter the physical man is felt to be a secondary, a subordinate, an instrument through whom the spiritual man works; and the spiritual man is felt to be the real individuality. This is, in a sense, the attainment to full salvation and immortal life; yet it is not the final goal or resting place, but only the beginning of the greater way.

The means for this transfer are described as the weakening of the causes of bondage, and an understanding of the method of passing from the one consciousness to the other. The first may also be described as detach meet, and comes from the conquest of the delusion that the personal self is the real man. When that delusion abates and is held in check, the finer consciousness of the spiritual man begins to shine in the background of the mind. The transfer of the sense of individuality to this finer consciousness, and thus to the spiritual man, then becomes a matter of recollection, of attention; primarily, a matter of taking a deeper interest in the life and doings of the spiritual man, than in the pleasures or occupations of the personality. Therefore it is said: "Lay not up for yourselves treasures upon earth, where moth and rust cloth corrupt, and where thieves break through and steal: but lay up for yourselves treasures in heaven, where neither moth nor rust cloth corrupt, and where thieves do not break through nor steal: for where your treasure is, there will your heart be also."

39. Through mastery of the upward-life comes freedom from the dangers of water, morass, and thorny places, and the power of ascension is gained.

Here is one of the sentences, so characteristic of this author, and, indeed, of the Eastern spirit, in which there is an obvious exterior meaning, and, within this, a clear interior meaning, not quite so obvious, but far more vital.

The surface meaning is, that by mastery of a certain power, called here the upward-life, and akin to levitation, there comes the ability to walk on water, or to pass over thorny places without wounding the feet.

But there is a deeper meaning. When we speak of the disciple's path as a path of thorns, we use a symbol; and the same symbol is used here. The upward-life means something more than the power, often manifested in abnormal psychical experiences, of levitating the physical body, or near-by physical objects. It means the strong power of aspiration, of upward will, which first builds, and then awakes the spiritual man, and finally transfers the conscious individuality to him; for it is he who passes safely over the waters of death and rebirth, and is not pierced by the thorns in the path. Therefore it is said that he who would tread the path of power must look for a home in the air, and afterwards in the ether.

Of the upward-life, this is written in the Katha Upanishad: "A hundred and one are the heart's channels; of these one passes to the crown. Going up this, he comes to the immortal." This is the power of ascension spoken of in the Sutra.

40. By mastery of the binding-life comes radiance.

In the Upanishads, it is said that this binding-life unites the upward-life to the downward-life, and these lives have their analogies in the "vital breaths" in the body. The thought in the text seems to be, that, when the personality is brought thoroughly under control of the spiritual man, through the life-currents which bind them together, the personality is endowed with a new force, a strong personal magnetism, one might call it, such as is often an appanage of genius.

But the text seems to mean more than this and to have in view the "vesture of the colour of the sun" attributed by the Upanishads to the spiritual man; that vesture which a disciple has thus described: "The Lord shall change our vile body, that it may be fashioned like unto his glorious body"; perhaps "body of radiance" would better translate the Greek.

In both these passages, the teaching seems to be, that the body of the full-grown spiritual man is radiant or luminous,-for those at least, who have anointed their eyes wit! eye-salve, so that they see.

41. From perfectly concentrated Meditation on the correlation of hearing and the ether, comes the power of spiritual hearing.

Physical sound, we are told, is carried by the air, or by water, iron, or some medium on the same plane of substance. But then is a finer hearing, whose medium of transmission would seem to be the ether; perhaps no that ether which carries light, heat and magnetic waves, but, it may be, the far finer ether through which the power of gravity works. For, while light or heat or magnetic waves, travelling from the sun to the earth, take eight minutes for the journey, it is mathematically certain that the pull of gravitation does not take as much as eight seconds, or even the eighth of a second. The pull of gravitation travels, it would seem "as quick as thought"; so it may well be that, in thought transference or telepathy, the thoughts travel by the same way, carried by the same "thought-swift" medium.

The transfer of a word by telepathy is the simplest and earliest form of the "divine hearing" of the spiritual man; as that power grows, and as, through perfectly concentrated Meditation, the spiritual man comes into more complete mastery of it, he grows able to hear and clearly distinguish the speech of the great Companions, who counsel and comfort him on his way. They may speak to him either in wordless thoughts, or in perfectly definite words and sentences.

42. By perfectly concentrated Meditation em the correlation of the body with the ether, and by thinking of it as light as thistle-down, will come the power to traverse the ether.

It has been said that he who would tread the path of power must look for a home in the air, and afterwards in the ether. This would seem to mean, besides the constant injunction to detachment, that he must be prepared to inhabit first a psychic, and then an etheric body; the former being the body of dreams; the latter, the body of the spiritual man, when he wakes up on the other side of dreamland. The gradual accustoming of the consciousness to its new etheric vesture, its gradual acclimatization, so to speak, in the etheric body of the spiritual man, is what our text seems to contemplate.

43. When that condition of consciousness is reached, which is far-reaching and not confined to the body, which is outside the body and not conditioned by it, then the veil which conceals the light is worn away.

Perhaps the best comment on this is afforded by the words of Paul: "I knew a man in Christ above fourteen years ago, (whether in the body, I cannot tell; or whether out of the body, I cannot tell: God knoweth;) such a one caught up to the third heaven. And I knew such a man, (whether in the body, or out of the body, I cannot tell: God knoweth;) how that he was caught up into paradise, and heard unspeakable [or, unspoken] words, which it is not lawful for a man to utter."

The condition is, briefly, that of the awakened spiritual man, who sees and hears beyond the veil.

44. Mastery of the elements comes from perfectly concentrated Meditation on their five forms: the gross, the elemental, the subtle, the inherent, the purposive.

These five forms are analogous to those recognized by modern physics: solid, liquid, gaseous, radiant and ionic. When the piercing vision of the awakened spiritual man is directed to the forms of matter, from within, as it were, from behind the scenes, then perfect mastery over the "beggarly elements" is attained. This is, perhaps, equivalent to the injunction: "Inquire of the earth, the air, and the water, of the secrets they hold for you. The development of your inner senses will enable you to do this."

45. Thereupon will come the manifestation of the atomic and other powers, which are the endowment of the body, together with its unassailable force.

The body in question is, of course, the etheric body of the spiritual man. He is said to possess eight powers: the atomic, the power of assimilating himself with the nature of the atom, which will, perhaps, involve the power to disintegrate material forms; the power of levitation; the power of limitless extension; the power of boundless reach, so that, as the commentator says, "he can touch the moon with the tip of his finger"; the power to accomplish his will; the power of gravitation, the correlative of levitation; the power of command; the power of creative will. These are the endowments of the spiritual man. Further, the spiritual body is unassailable. Fire burns it not, water wets it not, the sword cleaves it not, dry winds parch it not. And, it is said, the spiritual man can impart something of this quality and temper to his bodily vesture.

46. Shapeliness, beauty, force, the temper of the diamond: these are the endowments of that body.

The spiritual man is shapely, beautiful strong, firm as the diamond. Therefore it is written: "These things saith the Son of God, who hath his eyes like unto a flame of fire, and his feet are like fine brass: He that overcometh and keepeth my works unto the end, to him will I give power over the nations: and he shall rule them with a rod of iron; and I will give him the morning star."

47. Mastery over the powers of perception and action comes through perfectly concentrated Meditation on their fivefold forms; namely, their power to grasp their distinctive nature, the element of self-consciousness in them, their inherence, and their purposiveness.

Take, for example, sight. This possesses, first, the power to grasp, apprehend, perceive; second, it has its distinctive form of perception; that is, visual perception; third, it always carries with its operations self-consciousness, the thought: "I perceive"; fourth sight has the power of extension through the whole field of vision, even to the utmost star; fifth, it is used for the purposes of the Seer. So with the other senses. Perfectly concentrated Meditation on each sense, a viewing it from behind and within, as is possible for the spiritual man, brings a mastery of the scope and true character of each sense, and of the world on which they report collectively.

48. Thence comes the power swift as thought, independent of instruments, and the mastery over matter.

We are further enumerating the endowments of the spiritual man. Among these is the power to traverse space with the swiftness of thought, so that whatever place the spiritual man thinks of, to that he goes, in that place he already is. Thought has now become his means of locomotion. He is, therefore, independent of instruments, and can bring his force to bear directly, wherever he wills.

49. When the spiritual man is perfectly disentangled from the psychic body, he attains to mastery over all things and to a knowledge of all.

The spiritual man is enmeshed in the web of the emotions; desire, fear, ambition, passion; and impeded by the mental forms of separateness and materialism. When these meshes are sundered, these obstacles completely overcome, then the spiritual man stands forth in his own wide world, strong, mighty, wise. He uses divine powers, with a divine scope and energy, working together with divine Companions. To such a one it is said: "Thou art now a disciple, able to stand, able to hear, able to see, able to speak, thou hast conquered desire and attained to self-knowledge, thou hast seen thy soul in its bloom and recognized it, and heard the voice of the silence."

50. By absence of all self-indulgence at this point, when the seeds of bondage to sorrow are destroyed, pure spiritual being is attained.

The seeking of indulgence for the personal self, whether through passion or ambition, sows the seed of future sorrow. For this self indulgence of the personality is a double sin against the real; a sin against the cleanness of life, and a sin against the universal being, which permits no exclusive particular good, since, in the real, all spiritual possessions are held in common. This twofold sin brings its reacting punishment, its confining bondage to sorrow. But ceasing from self-indulgence brings purity, liberation, spiritual life.

51. There should be complete overcoming of allurement or pride in the invitations of the different realms of life, lest attachment to things evil arise once more.

The commentator tells us that disciples, seekers for union, are of four degrees: first, those who are entering the path; second, those who are in the realm of allurements; third, those who have won the victory over matter and the senses; fourth, those who stand firm in pure spiritual life. To the second, especially, the caution in the text is addressed. More modern teachers would express the same truth by a warning against the delusions and fascinations of the psychic realm, which open around the disciple, as he breaks through into the unseen worlds. These are the dangers of the anteroom. Safety lies in passing on swiftly into the inner chamber. "Him that overcometh will I make a pillar in the temple of my God, and he shall go no more out."

52. From perfectly concentrated Meditation on the divisions of time and their succession comes that wisdom which is born of discernment.

The Upanishads say of the liberated that "he has passed beyond the triad of time"; he no longer sees life as projected into past, present and future, since these are forms of the mind; but beholds all things spread out in the quiet light of the Eternal. This would seem to be the same thought, and to point to that clear-eyed spiritual perception which is above time; that wisdom born of the unveiling of Time's delusion. Then shall the disciple live neither in the present nor the future, but in the Eternal.

53. Hence comes discernment between things which are of like nature, not distinguished by difference of kind, character or position.

Here, as also in the preceding Sutra, we are close to the doctrine that distinctions of order, time and space are creations of the mind; the threefold prism through which the real object appears to us distorted and refracted. When the prism is withdrawn, the object returns to its primal unity, no longer distinguishable by the mind, yet clearly knowable by that high power of spiritual discernment, of illumination, which is above the mind.

54. The wisdom which is born of discernment is starlike; it discerns all things, and all conditions of things, it discerns without succession: simultaneously.

That wisdom, that intuitive, divining power is starlike, says the commentator, because it shines with its own light, because it rises on high, and illumines all things. Nought is hid from it, whether things past, things present, or things to come; for it is beyond the threefold form of time, so that all things are spread before it together, in the single light of the divine. This power has been beautifully described by Columba: "Some there are, though very few, to whom Divine grace has granted this: that they can clearly and most distinctly see, at one and the same moment, as though under one ray of the sun, even the entire circuit of the whole world with its surroundings of ocean and sky, the inmost part of their mind being marvellously enlarged."

55. When the vesture and the spiritual man are alike pure, then perfect spiritual life is attained.

The vesture, says the commentator, must first be washed pure of all stains of passion and darkness, and the seeds of future sorrow must be burned up utterly. Then, both the vesture and the wearer of the vesture being alike pure, the spiritual man enters into perfect spiritual life.

INTRODUCTION TO BOOK IV

The third book of the Sutras has fairly completed the history of the birth and growth of the spiritual man, and the enumeration of his powers; at least so far as concerns that first epoch in his immortal life, which immediately succeeds, and supersedes, the life of the natural man.

In the fourth book, we are to consider what one might call the mechanism of salvation, the ideally simple working of cosmic law which brings the spiritual man to birth, growth, and fulness of power, and prepares him for the splendid, toilsome further stages of his great journey home.

The Sutras are here brief to obscurity; only a few words, for example, are given to the great triune mystery and illusion of Time; a phrase or two indicates the sweep of some universal law. Yet it is hoped that, by keeping our eyes fixed on the spiritual man, remembering that he is the hero of the story, and that all that is written concerns him and his adventures, we may be able to find our way through this thicket of tangled words, and keep in our hands the clue to the mystery.

The last part of the last book needs little introduction. In a sense, it is the most important part of the whole treatise, since it unmasks the nature of the personality, that psychical "mind," which is the wakeful enemy of all who seek to tread the path. Even now, we can hear it whispering the doubt whether that can be a good path, which thus sets "mind" at defiance.

If this, then, be the most vital and fundamental part of the teaching, should it not stand at the very beginning? It may seem so at first; but had it stood there, we should not have comprehended it. For he who would know the doctrine must lead the life, doing the will of his Father which is in Heaven.

BOOK IV

1. Psychic and spiritual powers may be inborn, or they may be gained by the use of drugs, or by incantations, or by fervour, or by Meditation.

Spiritual powers have been enumerated and described in the preceding sections. They are the normal powers of the spiritual man, the antetype, the divine edition, of the powers of the natural man. Through these powers, the spiritual man stands, sees, hears, speaks, in the spiritual world, as the physical man stands, sees, hears, speaks in the natural world.

There is a counterfeit presentment of the spiritual man, in the world of dreams, a shadow lord of shadows, who has his own dreamy powers of vision, of hearing, of movement; he has left the natural without reaching the spiritual. He has set forth from the shore, but has not gained the further verge of the river. He is borne along by the stream, with no foothold on either shore. Leaving the actual, he has fallen short of the real, caught in the limbo of vanities and delusions. The cause of this aberrant phantasm is always the worship of a false, vain self, the lord of dreams, within one's own breast. This is the psychic man, lord of delusive and bewildering psychic powers.

Spiritual powers, like intellectual or artistic gifts, may be inborn: the fruit, that is, of seeds planted and reared with toil in a former birth. So also the powers of the psychic man may be inborn, a delusive harvest from seeds of delusion.

Psychical powers may be gained by drugs, as poverty, shame, debasement may be gained by the self-same drugs. In their action, they are baneful, cutting the man off from consciousness of the restraining power of his divine nature, so that his forces break forth exuberant, like the laughter of drunkards, and he sees and hears things delusive. While sinking, he believes that he has risen; growing weaker, he thinks himself full of strength; beholding illusions, he takes them to be true. Such are the powers gained by drugs; they are wholly psychic, since the real powers, the spiritual, can never be so gained.

Incantations are affirmations of half-truths concerning spirit and matter, what is and what is not, which work upon the mind and slowly build up a wraith of powers and a delusive well-being. These, too, are of the psychic realm of dreams.

Lastly, there are the true powers of the spiritual man, built up and realized in Meditation, through reverent obedience to spiritual law, to the pure conditions of being, in the divine realm.

2. The transfer of powers from one venture to another comes through the flow of the natural creative forces.

Here, if we can perceive it, is the whole secret of spiritual birth, growth and life Spiritual being, like all being, is but an expression of the Self, of the inherent power and being of Atma. Inherent in the Self are consciousness and will, which have, as their lordly heritage, the wide sweep of the universe throughout eternity, for the Self is one with the Eternal. And the consciousness of the Self may make itself manifest as seeing, hearing, tasting, feeling, or whatsoever perceptive powers there may be, just as the white sunlight may divide into many-coloured rays. So may the will of the Self manifest itself in the uttering of words, or in handling, or in moving, and whatever powers of action there are throughout the seven worlds. Where the Self is, there will its powers be. It is but a question of the vesture through which these powers shall shine forth. And wherever the consciousness and desire of the ever-creative Self are fixed, there will a vesture be built up; where the heart is, there will the treasure be also.

Since through ages the desire of the Self has been toward the natural world, wherein the Self sought to mirror himself that he might know himself, therefore a vesture of natural elements came into being, through which blossomed forth the Self's powers of perceiving and of will: the power to see, to hear, to speak, to walk, to handle; and when the Self, thus come to self-consciousness, and, with it, to a knowledge of his imprisonment, shall set his desire on the divine and real world, and raise his consciousness thereto, the spiritual vesture shall be built up for him there, with its expression of his inherent powers. Nor will migration thither be difficult for the Self, since the divine is no strange or foreign land for him, but the house of his home, where he dwells from everlasting.

3. The apparent, immediate cause is not the true cause of the creative nature-powers; but, like the husbandman in his field, it takes obstacles away.

The husbandman tills his field, breaking up the clods of earth into fine mould, penetrable to air and rain; he sows his seed, carefully covering it, for fear of birds and the wind; he waters the seed-laden earth, turning the little rills from the irrigation tank now this way and that, removing obstacles from the channels, until the even How of water vitalizes the whole field. And so the plants germinate and grow, first the blade, then the ear, then the full corn in the ear. But it is not the husbandman who makes them grow. It is, first, the miraculous plasmic power in the grain of seed, which brings forth after its kind; then thc alchcmy of sunlight which, in presence of the green colouring matter of the leaves, gathers hydrogen from the water and carbon from the gases in the air, and mingles them in the hydro-carbons of plant growth; and, finally, the wholly occult vital powers of the plant itself, stored up through ages, and flowing down from the primal sources of life. The husbandman but removes the obstacles. He plants and waters, but God gives the increase.

So with the finer husbandman of diviner fields. He tills and sows, but the growth of the spiritual man comes through the surge and flow of divine, creative forces and powers. Here, again, God gives the increase. The divine Self puts forth, for the manifestation of its powers, a new and finer vesture, the body of the spiritual man.

4. Vestures of consciousness are built up in conformity with the Boston of the feeling of selfhood.

The Self, says a great Teacher, in turn attaches itself to three vestures: first, to the physical body, then to the finer body, and thirdly to the causal body. Finally it stands forth radiant, luminous, joyous, as the Self.

When the Self attributes itself to the physical body, there arise the states of bodily consciousness, built up about the physical self.

When the Self, breaking through this first illusion, begins to see and feel itself in the finer body, to find selfhood there, then the states of consciousness of the finer body come into being; or, to speak exactly, the finer body and its states of consciousness arise and grow together.

But the Self must not dwell permanently there. It must learn to find itself in the causal body, to build up the wide and luminous fields of consciousness that belong to that.

Nor must it dwell forever there, for there remains the fourth state, the divine, with its own splendour and everlastingness.

It is all a question of the states of consciousness; all a question of raising the sense of selfhood, until it dwells forever in the Eternal.

5. In the different fields of manifestation, the Consciousness, though one, is the elective cause of many states of consciousness.

Here is the splendid teaching of oneness that lies at the heart of the Eastern wisdom. Consciousness is ultimately One, everywhere and forever. The Eternal, the Father, is the One Self of All Beings. And so, in each individual who is but a facet of that Self, Consciousness is One. Whether it breaks through as the dull fire of physical life, or the murky flame of the psychic and passional, or the radiance of the spiritual man, or the full glory of the Divine, it is ever the Light, naught but the

Light. The one Consciousness is the effective cause of all states of consciousness, on every plane.

6. Among states of consciousness, that which is born of Contemplation is free from the seed of future sorrow.

Where the consciousness breaks forth in the physical body, and the full play of bodily life begins, its progression carries with it inevitable limitations. Birth involves death. Meetings have their partings. Hunger alternates with satiety. Age follows on the heels of youth. So do the states of consciousness run along the circle of birth and death.

With the psychic, the alternation between prize and penalty is swifter. Hope has its shadow of fear, or it is no hope. Exclusive love is tortured by jealousy. Pleasure passes through deadness into pain. Pain's surcease brings pleasure back again. So here, too, the states of consciousness run their circle. In all psychic states there is egotism, which, indeed, is the very essence of the psychic; and where there is egotism there is ever the seed of future sorrow. Desire carries bondage in its womb.

But where the pure spiritual consciousness begins, free from self and stain, the ancient law of retaliation ceases; the penalty of sorrow lapses and is no more imposed. The soul now passes, no longer from sorrow to sorrow, but from glory to glory. Its growth and splendour have no limit. The good passes to better, best.

7. The works of followers after Union make neither for bright pleasure nor for dark pain The works of others make for pleasure or pain, or a mingling of these.

The man of desire wins from his works the reward of pleasure, or incurs the penalty of pain; or, as so often happens in life, his guerdon, like the passionate mood of the lover, is part pleasure and part pain. Works done with self-seeking bear within them the seeds of future sorrow; conversely, according to the proverb, present pain is future gain.

But, for him who has gone beyond desire, whose desire is set on the Eternal, neither pain to be avoided nor pleasure to be gained inspires his work. He fears no hell and desires no heaven. His one desire is, to know the will of the Father and finish His work. He comes directly in line with the divine Will, and works cleanly and immediately, without longing or fear. His heart dwells in the Eternal; all his desires are set on the Eternal.

8. From the force inherent in works comes the manifestation of those dynamic mind images which are conformable to the ripening out of each of these works.

We are now to consider the general mechanism of Karma, in order that we may pass on to the consideration of him who is free from Karma. Karma, indeed, is the concern of the personal man, of his bondage or freedom. It is the succession of the forces which built up the personal man, reproducing themselves in one personality after another.

Now let us take an imaginary case, to see how these forces may work out. Let us think of a man, with murderous intent in his heart, striking with a dagger at his enemy. He makes a red wound in his victim's breast; at the same instant he paints, in his own mind, a picture of that wound: a picture dynamic with all the fierce will-power he has put into his murderous blow. In other words he has made a deep wound in his own psychic body; and, when he comes to be born again, that body will become his outermost vesture, upon which, with its wound still there, bodily tissue will be built up. So the man will be born maimed, or with the predisposition to some mortal injury; he is unguarded at that point, and any trifling accidental blow will pierce the broken Joints of his psychic armour. Thus do the dynamic mind-images manifest themselves, coming to the surface, so that works done in the past may ripen and come to fruition.

9. Works separated by different nature, or place, or time, are brought together by the correspondence between memory and dynamic impression.

Just as, in the ripening out of mind-images into bodily conditions, the effect is brought about by the ray of creative force sent down by the Self, somewhat as the light of the magic lantern projects the details of a picture on the screen, revealing the hidden, and making secret things palpable and visible, so does this divine ray exercise a selective power on the dynamic mind-images, bringing together into one day of life the seeds gathered from many days. The memory constantly exemplifies this power; a passage of poetry will call up in the mind like passages of many poets, read at different times. So a prayer may call up many prayers.

In like manner, the same over-ruling selective power, which is a ray of the Higher Self, gathers together from different births and times and places those mind-images which are conformable, and may be grouped in the frame of a single life or a single event. Through this grouping, visible bodily conditions or outward circumstances are brought about, and by these the soul is taught and trained.

Just as the dynamic mind-images of desire ripen out in bodily conditions and circumstances, so the far more dynamic powers of aspiration, wherein the soul reaches toward the Eternal, have their fruition in a finer world, building the vesture of the spiritual man.

10. The series of dynamic mind-images is beginningless, because Desire is everlasting.

The whole series of dynamic mind-images, which make up the entire history of the personal man, is a part of the mechanism which the Self employs, to mirror itself in a reflection, to embody its powers in an outward form, to the end of self-expression, selfrealization, self-knowledge. Therefore the initial impulse behind these dynamic mind-images comes from the Self and is the descending ray of the Self; so that it cannot be said that there is any first member of the series of images, from which the rest arose. The impulse is beginningless, since it comes from the Self, which is from everlasting. Desire is not to cease; it is to turn to the Eternal, and so become aspiration.

11. Since the dynamic mind-images are held together by impulses of desire, by the wish for personal reward, by the substratum of mental habit, by the support of outer things desired; therefore, when these cease, the self reproduction of dynamic mind-images ceases.

We are still concerned with the personal life in its bodily vesture, and with the process whereby the forces which have upheld it are gradually transferred to the life of the spiritual man, and build up for him his finer vesture in a finer world.

How is the current to be changed? How is the flow of self-reproductive mind-images, which have built the conditions of life after life in this world of bondage, to be checked, that the time of imprisonment may come to an end, the day of liberation dawn?

The answer is given in the Sutra just translated. The driving-force is withdrawn and directed to the upbuilding of the spiritual body.

When the building impulses and forces are withdrawn, the tendency to manifest a new psychical body, a new body of bondage, ceases with them.

12. The difference between that which is past and that which is not yet come, according to their natures, depends on the difference of phase of their properties.

Here we come to a high and difficult matter, which has always been held to be of great moment in the Eastern wisdom:

the thought that the division of time into past, present and future is, in great measure, an illusion; that past, present, future all dwell together in the eternal Now.

The discernment of this truth has been held to be so necessarily a part of wisdom, that one of the names of the Enlightened is: "he who has passed beyond the three times: past, present, future."

So the Western Master said: "Before Abraham was, I am"; and again, "I am with you always, unto the end of the world"; using the eternal present for past and future alike. With the same purpose, the Master speaks of himself as "the alpha and the omega, the beginning and the end, the first and the last."

And a Master of our own days writes: "I feel even irritated at having to use these three clumsy words—past, present, and future. Miserable concepts of the objective phases of the subjective whole, they are about as ill adapted for the purpose, as an axe for finc carving."

In the eternal Now, both past and future are consummated.

Bjorklund, the Swedish philosopher, has well stated the same truth:

"Neither past nor future can exist to God; He lives undividedly, without limitations, and needs not, as man, to plot out his existence in a series of moments. Eternity then is not identical with unending time; it is a different form of existence, related to time as the perfect to the imperfect ... Man as an entity for himself must have the natural limitations for the part. Conceived by God, man is eternal in the divine sense, but conceived, by himself, man's eternal life is clothed in the limitations we call time. The eternal is a constant present without beginning or end, without past or future."

13. These properties, whether manifest or latent, are of the nature of the Three Potencies.

The Three Potencies are the three manifested modifications of the one primal material, which stands opposite to perceiving consciousness. These Three Potencies are called Substance, Force, Darkness; or viewed rather for their moral colouring, Goodness, Passion, Inertness. Every material manifestation is a projection of substance into the empty space of darkness. Every mental state is either good, or passional, or inert. So, whether subjective or objective, latent or manifest, all things that present themselves to the perceiving consciousness are compounded of these three. This is a fundamental doctrine of the Sankhya system.

14. The external manifestation of an object takes place when the transformations ore in the same phase.

We should be inclined to express the same law by saying, for example, that a sound is audible, when it consists of vibrations within the compass of the auditory nerve; that an object is visible, when either directly or by reflection, it sends forth luminiferous vibrations within the compass of the retina and the optic nerve. Vibrations below or above that compass make no impression at all, and the object remains invisible; as, for example, a kettle of boiling water in a dark room, though the kettle is sending forth heat vibrations closely akin to light.

So, when the vibrations of the object and those of the perceptive power are in the same phase, the external manifestation of the object takes place.

There seems to be a further suggestion that the appearance of an object in the "present," or its remaining hid in the "past," or "future," is likewise a question of phase, and, just as the range of vibrations perceived might be increased by the development of finer senses, so the perception of things past, and things to come, may be easy from a higher point of view.

15. The paths of material things and of states of consciousness are distinct, as is manifest from the fact that the

same object may produce different impressions in different minds.

Having shown that our bodily condition and circumstances depend on Karma, while Karma depends on perception and will, the sage recognizes the fact that from this may be drawn the false deduction that material things are in no wise different from states of mind. The same thought has occurred, and still occurs, to all philosophers; and, by various reasonings, they all come to the same wise conclusion; that the material world is not made by the mood of any human mind, but is rather the manifestation of the totality of invisible Being, whether we call this Mahat, with the ancients, or Ether, with the moderns.

16. Nor do material objects depend upon a single mind, for how could they remain objective to others, if that mind ceased to think of them?

This is but a further development of the thought of the preceding Sutra, carrying on the thought that, while the universe is spiritual, yet its material expression is ordered, consistent, ruled by law, not subject to the whims or affirmations of a single mind. Unwelcome material things may be escaped by spiritual growth, by rising to a realm above them, and not by denying their existence on their own plane. So that our system is neither materialistic, nor idealistic in the extreme sense, but rather intuitional and spiritual, holding that matter is the manifestation of spirit as a whole, a reflection or externalization of spirit, and, like spirit, everywhere obedient to law. The path of liberation is not through denial of matter but through denial of the wills of self, through obedience, and that aspiration which builds the vesture of the spiritual man.

17. An object is perceived, or not perceived, according as the mind is, or is not, tinged with the colour of the object.

The simplest manifestation of this is the matter of attention. Our minds apprehend what they wish to apprehend; all else passes unnoticed, or, on the other hand, we perceive what we resent, as, for example, the noise of a passing train; while others, used to the sound, do not notice it at all.

But the deeper meaning is, that out of the vast totality of objects ever present in the universe, the mind perceives only those which conform to the hue of its Karma. The rest remain unseen, even though close at hand.

This spiritual law has been well expressed by Emerson:

"Through solidest eternal things the man finds his road as if they did not subsist, and does not once suspect their being. As soon as he needs a new object, suddenly he beholds it, and no longer attempts to pass through it, but takes another way. When he has exhausted for the time the nourishment to be drawn from any one person or thing, that object is withdrawn from his observation, and though still in his immediate neighbourhood, he does not suspect its presence. Nothing is dead. Men feign themselves dead, and endure mock funerals and mournful obituaries, and there they stand looking out of the window, sound and well, in some new and strange disguise. Jesus is not dead, he is very well alive: nor John, nor Paul, nor Mahomet, nor Aristotle; at times we believe we have seen them all, and could easily tell the names under which they go."

18. The movements of the psychic nature are perpetually objects of perception, since the Spiritual Man, who is the lord of them, remains unchanging.

Here is teaching of the utmost import, both for understanding and for practice.

To the psychic nature belong all the ebb and flow of emotion, all hoping and fearing, desire and hate: the things that make the multitude of men and women deem themselves happy or miserable. To it also belong the measuring and comparing, the doubt and questioning, which, for the same multitude, make up mental life. So that there results the emotion-soaked personality, with its dark and narrow view of life: the shivering, terror driven personality that is life itself for all but all of mankind.

Yet the personality is not the true man, not the living soul at all, but only a spectacle which the true man observes. Let us under stand this, therefore, and draw ourselves up inwardly to the height of the Spiritual Man, who, standing in the quiet light of the Eternal, looks down serene upon this turmoil of the outer life.

One first masters the personality, the "mind," by thus looking down on it from above, from within; by steadily watching its ebb and flow, as objective, outward, and therefore not the real Self. This standing back is the first step, detachment. The second, to maintain the vantage-ground thus gained, is recollection.

19. The Mind is not self-luminous, since it can be seen as an object.

This is a further step toward overthrowing the tyranny of the "mind": the psychic nature of emotion and mental measuring. This psychic self, the personality, claims to be absolute, asserting that life is for it and through it; it seeks to impose on the whole being of man its narrow, materialistic, faithless view of life and the universe; it would clip the wings of the soaring Soul. But the Soul dethrones the tyrant, by perceiving and steadily affirming that the psychic self is no true self at all, not self-luminous, but only an object of observation, watched by the serene eyes of the Spiritual Man.

20. Nor could the Mind at the same time know itself and things external to it.

The truth is that the "mind" knows neither external things nor itself. Its measuring and analyzing, its hoping and fearing, hating and desiring, never give it a true measure of life, nor any sense of real values. Ceaselessly active, it never really attains to knowledge; or, if we admit its knowledge, it ever falls short of wisdom, which comes only through intuition, the vision of the Spiritual Man.

Life cannot be known by the "mind," its secrets cannot be learned through the "mind." The proof is, the ceaseless strife and contradiction of opinion among those who trust in the mind. Much less can the "mind" know itself, the more so, because it is pervaded by the illusion that it truly knows, truly is.

True knowledge of the "mind" comes, first, when the Spiritual Man, arising, stands detached, regarding the "mind" from above, with quiet eyes, and seeing it for the tangled web of psychic forces that it truly is. But the truth is divined long before it is clearly seen, and then begins the long battle of the "mind," against the Real, the "mind" fighting doggedly, craftily, for its supremacy.

21. If the Mind be thought of as seen by another more inward Mind, then there would be an endless series of perceiving Minds, and a confusion of memories.

One of the expedients by which the "mind" seeks to deny and thwart the Soul, when it feels that it is beginning to be circumvented and seen through, is to assert that this seeing is the work of a part of itself, one part observing the other, and thus leaving no need nor place for the Spiritual Man.

To this strategy the argument is opposed by our philosopher, that this would be no true solution, but only a postponement of the solution. For we should have to find yet another part of the mind to view the first observing part, and then another to observe this, and so on, endlessly.

The true solution is, that the Spiritual Man looks down upon the psychic nature, and observes it; when he views the psychic pictures gallery, this is "memory," which would be a hopeless, inextricable confusion, if we thought of one part of the "mind," with its memories, viewing another part, with memories of its own.

The solution of the mystery lies not in the "mind" but beyond it, in the luminous life of the risen Lord, the Spiritual Man.

22. When the psychical nature takes on the form of the spiritual intelligence, by reflecting it, then the Self becomes conscious of its own spiritual intelligence.

We are considering a stage of spiritual life at which the psychical nature has been cleansed and purified. Formerly, it reflected in its plastic substance the images of the earthy; purified now, it reflects the image of the heavenly, giving the spiritual intelligence a visible form. The Self, beholding that visible form, in which its spiritual intelligence has, as it were, taken palpable shape, thereby reaches self-recognition, self-comprehension. The Self sees itself in this mirror, and thus becomes not only conscious, but self-conscious. This is, from one point of view, the purpose of the whole evolutionary process.

23. The psychic nature, taking on the colour of the Seer and of things seen, leads to the perception of all objects.

In the unregenerate man, the psychic nature is saturated with images of material things, of things seen, or heard, or tasted, or felt; and this web of dynamic images forms the ordinary material and driving power of life. The sensation of sweet things tasted clamours to be renewed, and drives the man into effort to obtain its renewal; so he adds image to image, each dynamic and importunate, piling up sin's intolerable burden.

Then comes regeneration, and the washing away of sin, through the fiery, creative power of the Soul, which burns out the stains of the psychic vesture, purifying it as gold is refined in the furnace. The suffering of regeneration springs from this indispensable purifying.

Then the psychic vesture begins to take on the colour of the Soul, no longer stained, but suffused with golden light; and the man red generate gleams with the radiance of eternity. Thus the Spiritual Man puts on fair raiment; for of this cleansing it is said: Though your sins be as scarlet, they shall be white as snow; though they be as crimson, they shall be as wool.

24. The psychic nature, which has been printed with mind-images of innumerable material things, exists now for the Spiritual Man, building for him.

The "mind," once the tyrant, is now the slave, recognized as outward, separate, not Self, a well-trained instrument of the Spiritual Man.

For it is not ordained for the Spiritual Man that, finding his high realm, he shall enter altogether there, and pass out of the vision of mankind. It is true that he dwells in heaven, but he also dwells on earth. He has angels and archangels, the hosts of the just made perfect, for his familiar friends, but he has at the same time found a new kinship with the prone children of men, who stumble and sin in the dark. Finding sinlessness, he finds also that the world's sin and shame are his, not to share, but to atone; finding kinship with angels, he likewise finds his part in the toil of angels, the toil for the redemption of the world.

For this work, he, who now stands in the heavenly realm, needs his instrument on earth; and this instrument he finds, ready to his hand, and fitted and perfected by the very struggles he has waged against it, in the personality, the "mind," of the personal man. This once tyrant is now his servant and perfect ambassador, bearing witness, before men, of heavenly things and even in this present world doing the will and working the works of the Father.

25. For him who discerns between the Mind and the Spiritual Man, there comes perfect fruition of the longing after the real being of the Self.

How many times in the long struggle have the Soul's aspirations seemed but a hopeless, impossible dream, a madman's counsel of perfection. Yet every finest, most impossible aspiration shall be realized, and ten times more than realized, once the long, arduous fight against the "mind," and the mind's worldview is won. And then it will be seen that unfaith and despair were but weapons of the "mind," to daunt the Soul, and put off the day when the neck of the "mind" shall be put under the foot of the Soul.

Have you aspired, well-nigh hopeless, after immortality? You shall be paid by entering the immortality of God.

Have you aspired, in misery and pain, after consoling, healing love? You shall be made a dispenser of the divine love of God Himself to weary souls.

Have you sought ardently, in your day of feebleness, after power? You shall wield power immortal, infinite, with God working the works of God.

Have you, in lonely darkness, longed for companionship and consolation? You shall have angels and archangels for your friends, and all the immortal hosts of the Dawn.

These are the fruits of victory. Therefore overcome. These are the prizes of regeneration. Therefore die to self, that you may rise again to God.

26. Thereafter, the whole personal being bends toward illumination, toward Eternal Life.

This is part of the secret of the Soul, that salvation means, not merely that a soul shall be cleansed and raised to heaven, but that the whole realm of the natural powers shall be redeemed, building up, even in this present world, the kingly figure of the Spiritual Man.

The traditions of the ages are full of his footsteps; majestic, uncomprehended shadows, myths, demi-gods, fill the memories of all the nobler peoples. But the time cometh, when he shall be known, no longer demi-god, nor myth, nor shadow, but the ever-present Redeemer, working amid men for the life and cleansing of all souls.

27. In the internals of the batik, other thoughts will arise, through the impressions of the dynamic mind-images.

The battle is long and arduous. Let there be no mistake as to that. Go not forth to this battle without counting the cost. Ages have gone to the strengthening of the foe. Ages of conflict must be spent, ere the foe, wholly conquered, becomes the servant, the Soul's minister to mankind.

And from these long past ages, in hours when the contest flags, will come new foes, mind-born children springing up to fight for mind, reinforcements coming from forgotten years, forgotten lives. For once this conflict is begun, it can be ended only by sweeping victory, and unconditional, unreserved surrender of the vanquished.

28. These are to be overcome as it was taught that hindrances should be overcome.

These new enemies and fears are to be overcome by ceaselessly renewing the fight, by a steadfast, dogged persistence, whether in victory or defeat, which shall put the stubbornness of the rocks to shame. For the Soul is older than all things, and invincible; it is of the very nature of the Soul to be unconquerable.

Therefore fight on, undaunted; knowing that the spiritual will, once awakened, shall, through the effort of the contest, come to its full strength; that ground gained can be held permanently; that great as is the dead-weight of the adversary, it is yet measurable, while the Warrior who fights for you, for whom you fight, is, in might, immeasurable, invincible, everlasting.

29. He who, after he has attained, is wholly free from self, reaches the essence of all that can be known, gathered together like a cloud. This is the true spiritual consciousness.

It has been said that, at the beginning of the way, we must kill out ambition, the great curse, the giant weed which grows as strongly in the heart of the devoted disciple as in the man of desire. The remedy is sacrifice of self, obedience, humility; that purity of heart which gives the vision of God. Thereafter, he who has attained is wrapt about with the essence of all that can be known, as with a cloud; he has that perfect illumination which is the true spiritual consciousness. Through obedience to the will of God, he comes into oneness of being with God; he is initiated into God's view of the universe, seeing all life as God sees it.

30. Thereon comes surcease from sorrow and the burden of toil.

Such a one, it is said, is free from the bond of Karma, from the burden of toil, from that debt to works which comes from works done in self-love and desire. Free from self-will, he is free from sorrow, too, for sorrow comes from the fight of self-will against the divine will, through the correcting stress of the divine will, which seeks to counteract the evil wrought by disobedience. When the conflict with the divine will ceases, then sorrow ceases, and he who has grown into obedience, thereby enters into joy.

31. When all veils are rent, all stains washed away, his knowledge becomes infinite; little remains for him to know.

The first veil is the delusion that thy soul is in some permanent way separate from the great Soul, the divine Eternal.

When that veil is rent, thou shalt discern thy oneness with everlasting Life. The second veil is the delusion of enduring separateness from thy other selves, whereas in truth the soul that is in them is one with the soul that is in thee. The world's sin and shame are thy sin and shame: its joy also.

These veils rent, thou shalt enter into knowledge of divine things and human things. Little will remain unknown to thee.

32. Thereafter comes the completion of the series of transformations of the three nature potencies, since their purpose is attained.

It is a part of the beauty and wisdom of the great Indian teachings, the Vedanta and the Yoga alike, to hold that all life exists for the purposes of Soul, for the making of the spiritual man. They teach that all nature is an orderly process of evolution, leading up to this, designed for this end, existing only for this: to bring forth and perfect the Spiritual Man. He is the crown of evolution: at his coming, the goal of all development is attained.

33. The series of transformations is divided into moments. When the series is completed, time gives place to duration.

There are two kinds of eternity, says the commentary: the eternity of immortal life, which belongs to the Spirit, and the eternity of change, which inheres in Nature, in all that is not Spirit. While we are content to live in and for Nature, in the Circle of Necessity, Sansara, we doom ourselves to perpetual change. That which is born must die, and that which dies must be reborn. It is change evermore, a ceaseless series of transformations.

But the Spiritual Man enters a new order; for him, there is no longer eternal change, but eternal Being. He has entered into the joy of his Lord. This spiritual birth, which makes him heir of the Everlasting, sets a term to change; it is the culmination, the crowning transformation, of the whole realm of change.

34. Pure spiritual life is, therefore, the inverse resolution of the potencies of Nature, which have emptied themselves of their value for the Spiritual man; or it is the return of the power of pure Consciousness to its essential form.

Here we have a splendid generalization, in which our wise philosopher finally reconciles the naturalists and the idealists, expressing the crown and end of his teaching, first in the terms of the naturalist, and then in the terms of the idealist.

The birth and growth of the Spiritual Man, and his entry into his immortal heritage, may be regarded, says our philosopher, either as the culmination of the whole process of natural evolution and involution, where "that which flowed from out the boundless deep, turns again home"; or it may be looked at, as the Vedantins look at it, as the restoration of pure spiritual Consciousness to its pristine and essential form. There is no discrepancy or conflict between these two views, which are but two accounts of the same thing. Therefore those who study the wise philosopher, be they naturalist or idealist, have no excuse to linger over dialectic subtleties or disputes. These things are lifted from their path, lest they should be tempted to delay over them, and they are left facing the path itself, stretching upward and onward from their feet to the everlasting hills, radiant with infinite Light.